FUN, FUNKY & FABULOUS

D1294938

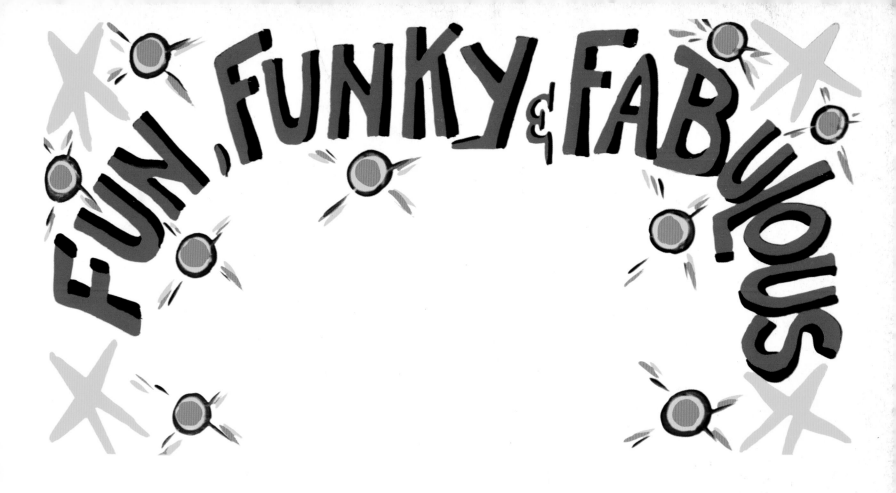

New Orleans' Casual Restaurant Recipes

Jyl Benson
Photography, Sam Hanna
Illustrations, Simon of New Orleans
Introduction, Liz Williams

PELICAN PUBLISHING COMPANY

GRETNA 2015

ISBN: 9781455620609
E-book ISBN: 9781455620616

Printed in Malaysia
Published by Pelican Publishing Company, Inc.
1000 Burmaster Street, Gretna, Louisiana 70053

On the Cover: Andouille Tots with Ranch Dipping Sauce, page 13
All cast iron products courtesy of Lodge Manufacturing

CONTENTS

Sea

Sweet

*"**Whatcha Know Good?**": A customary, old-school New Orleans Y'at-speak greeting akin to "Where Y'At,?" both of which are our butchered way of asking "What's up?," "Heard anything interesting lately? Tell Me," "What are you doing?" or "What's going on?"*

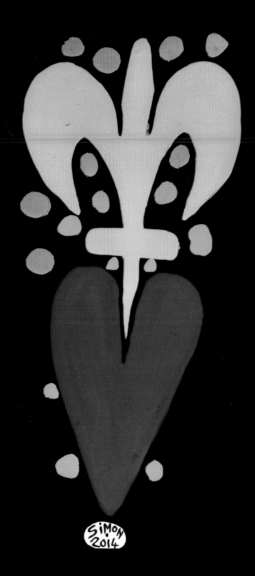

For my beautiful daughter, Cecilia McAlear, for compelling me to explore
the crossroads of Louisiana flavors and contemporary culinary sensibilities
and for my wise and patient husband, Andrew Fox, for absolutely everything every single day.

Introduction

The best thing about the cuisine of New Orleans is that it is alive. And because it is alive, it is always changing. While we seem to be able and willing to build new recipes on the past ones, we also keep moving forward. That means that our food is always being reinvented with changing times. And the exciting consequence of our willingness to change is that our cuisine remains fresh and reflective of the present. Our food always was and it remains fun, funky, and fabulous, not to mention delicious, inventive, and unique. And my friend Jyl Benson and the team that worked on this book capture the spirit of New Orleans and its food, and they serve it up with as much sass as can be found in the food itself.

The restaurant scene in New Orleans is full of great places to eat, each with its own charm and personality. We are known for our fine old establishments and older neighborhood favorites. But the new guard of New Orleans restaurants is full of quirky tastiness. Sometimes the out-of-the-way place is full of whimsy, and sometimes it is reflective of newly minted New Orleanians. And that diversity is one of the things that makes eating in this city such a taste treat. This book offers up such things as the Vietnamese inspired riff of a meal at MoPho as well as the more traditional reinvention of jambalaya at Crescent Plate. Different parts of town, different flavors, and all absolutely New Orleans.

Jyl's pick of recipes and the particular restaurants selected clearly represent the New Orleans of today. The book would make a handy guide to local neighborhoods and where to eat in each of them, besides being a great cookbook full of recipes that can actually be made in a home kitchen. And they are recipes that you will want to make. One look at the photographs and styling in Sam Hanna's photos and you cannot resist pulling out pots and pans and getting started. Not only does he reflect the goodness of those dishes he photographs, but Sam captures the way that the food itself reflects the languid yet spicy nature of the city. Nowhere else does the taste of the food so well reflect the sensuous nature of a place—the smells, the look, the sounds, the feel. This book puts the look of the city's food on your shelf.

The book's design by Michael Lauve works hand in glove with the recipes. The book is easy to read and easy on the eyes. It is stuffed full of information about the food, the restaurants, the history, and the neighborhoods, but it never feels crowded. Jyl has worked hard to make sure that each restaurant is presented in its own voice. And yet the whole book hangs together in the way that seemingly disparate neighborhoods and neighbors hang together to make a unique city like New Orleans.

Simon of New Orleans, artist, has added his more than a bit of whimsy to the book with his work on the cover and the art for the chapters. Just as his work is sprinkled throughout the book, his work is sprinkled around the city. He is just one more character who has worked to make this book represent the way people eat in New Orleans today.

Today's eaters in New Orleans want vegan choices as well as traditional fare. This book reflects the recipes and the places that can offer one or the other alternative. Cumin and Cilantro Pork Sausage Hand Pies from Brandon Blackwell show off the new Latino influences in the city with a nod to the traditional Louisiana hand pie. Louisiana Blue Crab Salad with Satsuma-Dijon Vinaigrette uses local blue crabs and local satsumas in the time-honored tradition of using what is at hand to make something delicious for the table. Miss Linda Green serves up Banana Bread Pudding with Extra-Boozy Rum Sauce and that makes me know that I am in old New Orleans eating a traditional dessert with bananas from the Port of New Orleans.

And whether it is Butter Bean Hummus, Molten Chocolate Cake with Chicory Coffee Sauce, or Fresh Watermelon Sorbet, these vegan options will ensure that taste does not take a back seat to the decision to forego animal products. Because the bottom line in a New Orleans restaurant is not décor. It is not people watching. It is taste.

I hope that New Orleans and its food continue to evolve and change with changing times. I hope that we never decide that only the foods that represent the past are the foods of New Orleans and that new ideas in food, new peoples, and new techniques have no place in our cuisine. I cannot imagine that that could happen except in some dark dystopia. And I think that this book will always represent the story of the cuisine of New Orleans in this day and time. It is irreverent. It is casual. It is seriously good. It is fun. It is delicious. My recommendation: Use this book and cook with it.

Liz Williams

August, 2014

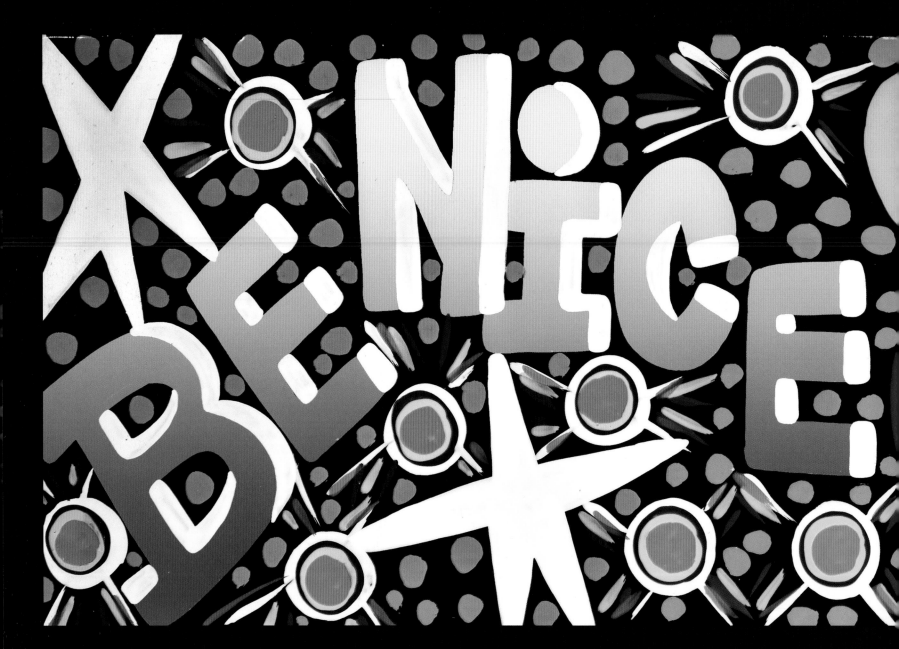

Start

Andouille Tots with Ranch Dipping Sauce

Chef Michael Nirenberg, Fulton Alley

Too cool for tater tots? Think not. These mind-numbingly delicious little morsels leave fans devoid of the sense God gave a cat to stop eating.

They. Are. That. Good. That said, they are also a bit of a pain to make: The potatoes must be brought to a boil in cold water three times in order to extract the starch properly so the shredded potato will remain "totted" as it fries.

So worth it.

Serves 4 to 6

- 2 cups small diced andouille sausage (about 1/2 pound)
- 3 large russet potatoes, peeled
- 1 tablespoon kosher salt
- 2 ounces sharp Cheddar cheese, cut into small cubes, about 1/4 inch
  Canola oil for frying
  Ranch Dipping Sauce (recipe follows)

Preheat the oven to 325°F.

Scatter the andouille on a baking sheet and cook until it has released all of its fat and the pieces are shriveled and hard but not burned, about twenty minutes. You should have about 1 cup. Drain the pieces thoroughly and set aside.

Place the peeled, uncut potatoes in a pot and cover with cold water. Bring to a boil over high heat. Drain the potatoes and rinse thoroughly to cool under cold water. Return the potatoes to the pot and cover with cold water. Bring to a boil over high heat. Drain the potatoes and rinse thoroughly to cool under cold water. Repeat this process one more time.

Feed each potato into a food processor fitted with the shredding blade. You may have to cut the potatoes a bit to fit them into the tube. Shred all potatoes. Put the shredded potatoes into a kitchen towel and squeeze out the excess liquid.

Mix together the potatoes, salt, and sausage. Using your hands, form tight 1-ounce (about the size of a walnut) balls or "tots" with the mixture. Force one piece of Cheddar into the center of each tot, taking care to ensure the cheese is fully encased. Set aside.

In a deep-fryer or heavy-bottomed pot, heat enough canola oil to come halfway up the sides of the pot to 375°F. Fry the tots until golden, about four to five minutes. Drain on paper towels. Serve with Ranch Dipping Sauce.

Ranch Dipping Sauce

The workhorse dipping sauce for crudités, onions rings, tater tots, anything. Change the flavor profile by substituting 1/4 teaspoon smoked chipotle chile powder or smoked paprika for the dried dill.

Makes about 2 cups

- 1 cup buttermilk
- 1/2 cup sour cream
- 1/2 cup mayonnaise
- 1/8 teaspoon dried dill
- 1/8 teaspoon garlic powder
- 1/4 teaspoon onion powder
- 1/4 cup chili vinegar or apple cider vinegar
- 1/2 tablespoon chopped parsley
- 1 teaspoon kosher salt
- 1 teaspoon black pepper

Combine buttermilk, sour cream, mayonnaise, dill, garlic powder, onion powder, vinegar, parsley, salt, and pepper. Refrigerate overnight to allow flavors to marry.

Whatcha Know Good?

Tulane grad school pals Shawn Barney and Kyle Brechtel devised a business plan for what later became Fulton Alley as part of their final practicum. Their off-the-wall downtown bowling alley evolved from an old bus barn/parking garage into a space lit by dazzling crystal chandeliers and adorned with local works from contemporary artists Mitchell Gaudet and Michel Varisco. And forget the fries and lite beer consumed in other sporting halls: The fun finger foods here are regionally rooted and upscale, and the craft cocktails from the team of Neal Bodenheimer and Kirk Estopinal, who launched the city's modern cocktail movement, are anything but same-old same-old.

Crispy Fried Oysters with MoPho Mayo and Pickled Blue Cheese Vinaigrette

Chef Michael Gulotta, MoPho

If oysters are not available, Chef Gulotta recommends substituting shucked little neck clams. Boiled, chilled shrimp could also be substituted for a very different (though still quite delicious) variation.

Serves 6 as an appetizer

1 quart Gulf oysters, drained
  Whites from 8 large eggs, lightly whisked
2 quarts Oyster Dredge *(recipe p. 118)*
  Canola oil for frying
  Salt to taste
2 cups MoPho Mayo *(recipe p. 118)*
2 cups Pickled Blue Cheese Vinaigrette *(recipe p. 118)*
2 small radishes, such as French Breakfast, Watermelon, or Easter Egg, very thinly sliced
  Fresh leaves of young basil and mint, picked

In a medium bowl, gently combine the oysters with egg whites. Add the Oyster Dredge to a large bowl; toss the oysters in the Oyster Dredge and coat evenly, shaking off any excess.

Heat two inches of canola oil to 360°F. in a deep fryer or a heavy-bottomed skillet over medium-high heat. Carefully drop the oysters, one at a time, into the oil and fry until golden in color, one to two minutes, turning if necessary. The oysters should be crispy on the outside but still juicy on the inside. With a slotted spoon, remove the oysters carefully and drain on paper towel-lined trays. Sprinkle the hot oysters with salt.

Serve the oysters atop a dollop of MoPho Mayo, drizzle with Pickled Blue Cheese Vinaigrette, and garnish with radish slices and small basil and mint leaves.

Whatcha Know Good?

A daring young chef makes a ballsy move, gives his place a ballsy name, and serves ballsy food. Go figure.

Michael Gulotta left his cushy position as chef de cuisine at John Besh's glamorous flagship, Restaurant August, to mortgage his life to the hilt and roll the dice on a spot in a strip mall next to a snowball stand and behind a Burger King. Opened in early 2014 with a name some found offensive, this casual hot spot marries Louisiana ingredients with the flavors of Southeast Asia. "It's where the Mekong Delta meets with Mississippi Delta." The name is a play on a slang phrase starting with "mother" and most often shouted under duress—like when you've smacked the crap out of your thumb with a hammer or had a near miss in traffic—and a bastardization on the proper pronunciation, "fuh," of Vietnamese pho.

Gulotta's gamble paid off, and the quirky name really suits the place where they pack the house for Sazerac bubble teas, pho made with things like hogs head cheese or duck confit, and bánh mì sandwiches stuffed with grilled Gulf shrimp and country ham.

Butter Bean Hummus with Rustic Roasted Garlic Bread (Vegan)

Langlois Culinary Crossroads

Large, creamy lima beans are best for this dish, but younger cooked green limas, kidney beans, flageolets, or while beans work well, too.

Serves 18 as an appetizer

- 1 pound dried or frozen butter beans (large limas)
- 1 tablespoon vegetable oil
- 1/4 cup diced onion
- 1 tablespoon minced garlic
- 3/4 cup olive oil, plus more for drizzling
- 1/4 teaspoon smoked paprika (pimenton de la vera), plus more for garnish
  Salt to taste
  Rustic Roasted Garlic Bread *(recipe p. 118)*
  Crudités, such as fresh radishes (optional)

Boil butter beans with enough water to cover in a medium saucepan until fork-tender, about thirty minutes, adding additional water as necessary. Drain and cool.

In a medium skillet over medium-high heat, sauté onion and garlic in oil until translucent.

Purée beans, onions, and garlic in a food processor until smooth. Slowly drizzle in olive oil. Season with smoked paprika and salt. Scrape mixture into a bowl, drizzle with olive oil, and dust with paprika. Serve with bread and crudités.

Whatcha Know Good?

Opened by Amy Cyrex Sins in November 2012, Langlois Culinary Crossroads offers hands-on and demonstration classes in authentic Cajun and Creole cuisines as well as modern interpretations of popular dishes and culinary tours.

Her inspiration for the cooking school/restaurant came from a bit of regional folklore many have come to accept as fact. "When French women first arrived in the New World with their native cooking techniques and no idea what to do with the things they found here, they became pretty angry. So, they revolted by banging pots and pans on Governor Jean-Baptiste de Bienville's lawn," Amy says.

The story has Bienville pressing his French-Canadian housekeeper, Madame Langlois, into service to introduce the new arrivals to the local produce, game, spices, and seafood as well as the techniques she had learned for cooking them from local natives. "Madame Langlois was the mother of Creole cuisine! In teaching those women, she had the first cooking school in North America!"

Crawtator-Crusted Gulf Oysters with Red Bean Gravy

Chef Chris Lusk, New Orleans

This recipe is an excellent example of how contemporary New Orleans chefs are inspired to take elements familiar to the city's definitive cuisine and present them in a fun new way.

The Crawtator breading would also make an excellent coating for pork chops or pounded chicken cutlets. Just toss the meat in an egg wash before coating. The wash is not necessary for oysters.

Serves 4 to 6

- 1 bag Zapp's Crawtator potato chips
- 2 cups instant potato flakes
- Creole seasoning to taste
- 1 cup panko bread crumbs
- 30 Gulf oysters, picked free of shells
- Oil for frying
- Salt and pepper to taste
- Red Bean Gravy (recipe follows)

Combine the chips, potato flakes, Creole seasoning, and bread crumbs in a food processor and process to a fine consistency.

In a deep fryer or heavy-bottomed pot, heat the oil to 350°F.

Dredge the oysters in the crumb mixture and fry until golden brown, about one to one and a half minutes. Drain fried oysters on paper towel and season with salt and pepper. Serve with Red Bean Gravy for dipping.

Whatcha Know Good?

Ron Zappe was an unlikely potato chip baron, having started his career as an industrial engineer in the Texas oil and gas industry—a successful career that went sour during the 1980s' oil bust. His astute entrepreneurial sense then turned to kettle-fried potato chips, and he wowed the masses with crisp, thickly cut chips kissed with Louisiana-centric flavors and fried in peanut oil at "the little chippery in Grammercy" in St. James Parish at the converted old Faucheux Chevrolet dealership on Airline Highway. The kettle-cooked chips caught on quickly, first locally, and then regionally and nationally, as snackers become addicted to varieties like the spicy Cajun Crawtators and ordered them shipped via a toll-free number before Internet purchases became an option.

Ron died unexpectedly in June 2010, leaving behind a proud legacy based on the quality of his products and the generosity of his spirit. Though Ron's little chippery was sold to Utz Quality Foods of Hanover, Pennsylvania, in 2011, those addictive chips are still produced in Grammercy.

Red Bean Gravy

This easy creation is fabulous as a dipping sauce for the oysters, or you can reheat it at medium-low for five minutes or so to intensify the color and serve it as a delicious cream soup.

Makes 1 1/2 quarts

- 1 stick unsalted butter
- 4 pieces sliced bacon, cut into small strips
- 1 onion, diced
- 2 garlic cloves, minced
- 2 stalks celery, diced
- 1 bell pepper, diced
- 1/4 cup all-purpose flour
- 2 cups half-and-half
- 2 cups chicken stock
- 2 cups cooked red beans
  (canned are fine, just drain and rinse them first)
- 1/4 tablespoon fresh thyme, chopped
- 1/4 tablespoon fresh oregano, chopped
- 1 tablespoon Louisiana-style hot sauce
- 1 tablespoon Worcestershire sauce
- 2 teaspoons Creole seasoning
- Salt and pepper to taste

Melt the butter in a heavy sauce pot over medium heat. Add the bacon and cook until it is crispy and the fat has rendered. Add the onions, garlic, celery, and bell pepper and cook until onions are translucent, eight to ten minutes.

Stir in the flour. Add the half-and-half and chicken stock. Bring to a simmer and reduce heat to low. Add the red beans and cook for twenty minutes on low heat. Add the thyme, oregano, hot sauce, Worcestershire sauce, and Creole seasoning. Use an immersion blender to purée the ingredients until smooth. Season to taste with salt and pepper.

Cumin and Cilantro Pork Sausage Hand Pies with Satsuma Crème Fraiche and Pickled Carrot Ribbons

Brandon Blackwell, Cleaver & Company Artisan Butchers/ The Splendid Pig

Brandon Blackwell, an artisan butcher with Cleaver & Company, created these richly flavorful savory hand pies that are perfect for a kick-ass party. Assemble the pies in advance—they freeze beautifully, too—and fry them off just before serving. They could also be fried in advance and re-crisped in the oven.

The heady dose of herbs and spices in the pies is really offset by the slightly sweet creaminess of the Satsuma Crème Fraiche, and the sweet/tart tang of the pickled carrots.

Makes 12 hand pies

2 1/2 pounds fresh ground pork
2 1/2 tablespoons chopped fresh garlic
  2/3 cup chopped fresh cilantro, plus additional for serving
  1/2 tablespoon ground toasted cumin
  1/2 teaspoon pink salt
    1 tablespoon fine sea salt
    1 teaspoon ground black pepper
    2 tablespoons dry white wine
       All-purpose flour as needed
       Pie Dough (recipe follows)
       Egg wash (2 eggs beaten with 2 tablespoons water)
       Oil for frying
       Satsuma Crème Fraiche (recipe follows)
       Pickled Carrot Ribbons (recipe p. 119)

Combine the pork, garlic, cilantro, cumin, salts, pepper, and wine in a mixing bowl. Blend well until the mixture becomes sticky.

Move the mixture into a large sauté pan over medium heat. Add small amounts of flour to the pan as needed to help absorb the fat that renders out, just until all of the meat is cooked through.

Remove from the heat. Cool. Correct seasoning as desired.

Divide the dough into 12 balls. Using a rolling pin, flatten each ball into a five-inch disc. Add a 1/4 cup of the sausage filling to the center of each. Brush the edges of each disc with egg wash, then fold the edges together to form a crescent. Crimp the edges of the pies with a fork.

Heat the oil in a deep fryer or Dutch oven to 350°F. Working in batches, fry the pies until they are golden and float to the top of the oil, turning as necessary.

Serve with Satsuma Crème Fraiche and Pickled Carrot Ribbons.

Pie Dough

Makes 12 hand pies

    3 cups all-purpose flour
1 1/2 teaspoons salt
  3/4 teaspoon baking powder
    6 tablespoons leaf lard
    1 egg
  3/4 cup whole milk

Sift together the flour, salt, and baking powder in a mixing bowl. Using two knives or a pastry cutter, cut in the leaf lard until the mixture resembles coarse meal.

In another bowl, beat the egg and milk together, then gradually add to the dry ingredients, using a fork to blend, until the dough comes together. It will be dry dough.

Dump the dough onto a floured surface and knead it into a ball. Refrigerate for at least thirty minutes.

Satsuma Crème Fraiche

Makes 2 cups

    1 cup heavy cream
    1 cup buttermilk
       Zest of 1 small ripe satsuma (may substitute a small tangerine or orange)

Combine the cream and the buttermilk. Cover and let sit, unrefrigerated, overnight. Add the zest and stir to thoroughly combine. Refrigerate for two hours or overnight to marry flavors before serving.

Will keep for one week in the refrigerator.

Louisiana Blue Crab Salad with Satsuma-Dijon Vinaigrette

Chef Ryan Hughes, Purloo

While the jumbo lump from Louisiana's blue Gulf crabs is the preference for this simple salad, it is a luxury item and costs more than the average household budget will support for a work-a-day meal. Feel free to substitute less-expensive white lump, crab claw meat, or whatever fresh crabmeat is native to your area.

Serves 8

- 1 pound jumbo lump Gulf crabmeat, carefully picked over for shells
  Dijon-Satsuma Vinaigrette (recipe follows)
  Salt and freshly ground pepper
- 4 ounces baby arugula
- 1/2 bulb fennel, very thinly julienned
- 3 satsumas or honey tangerines, peeled, pith and membranes removed, divided into supremes

Toss crabmeat with vinaigrette and season with salt and pepper. Divide arugula evenly among eight chilled salad plates; top each plate evenly with the fennel, then the crabmeat. Garnish each plate satsuma supremes.

Satsuma-Dijon Vinaigrette

Makes 2 cups

- 1 tablespoons minced shallot
- 1 teaspoon minced garlic
- 2 tablespoons chopped fresh tarragon
- 1 teaspoon chopped fresh thyme
- 2 tablespoons Dijon mustard
- 1/4 cup Steen's Cane Vinegar (may substitute malt or tarragon vinegar)
- 1/2 cup freshly squeezed satsuma or orange juice
- 1 cup light olive oil (do not use extra-virgin)

Whisk shallot, garlic, tarragon, thyme, mustard, vinegar, and juice to combine. Add the oil in thin rivulets, whisking constantly until emulsified.

Sizzling Gambas al Pil Pil
(Sautéed Shrimp in Smoked Paprika Cream)

Chef Glen Hogh, Vega Tapas Café

The smoked paprika lends a gorgeous vibrant color to the sauce.

This easy, impressive shrimp preparation is also highly versatile. Instead of ladling the shrimp and sauce into pastry shells, you could just spear the shrimp with toothpicks and set them out as a serve-yourself nibble. The mixture could also be served over rice or tossed with pasta for a quick, weeknight dinner with a Spanish accent.

Serves 6 as an appetizer

- 6 large store-bought puff pastry shells, such as Pepperidge Farm
- 5 tablespoons olive oil
- 18 large Gulf shrimp (about 3/4 pound), peeled and deveined
  Salt and freshly ground pepper to taste
- 6 garlic cloves, finely minced
- 1/2 teaspoon red pepper flakes
- 2 teaspoons smoked Spanish paprika (pimenton de la vera)
- 1 1/2 tablespoons fresh lemon juice
- 3 tablespoons dry sherry
- 1/3 cup heavy cream
- 3 tablespoons chopped fresh flat-leaf parsley

Heat puff pastry shells in a toaster oven on low heat.

Meanwhile, in a sauté pan over medium-high heat, warm the olive oil. Season shrimp with salt and pepper. Add the shrimp, garlic, red pepper flakes, and paprika to the hot pan and sauté until the shrimp just begin to turn pink, about two minutes on each side. Deglaze the pan with the lemon juice and sherry and scrape the browned bits from the bottom of the pan. Stir in the cream and reduce for three minutes. Remove the pan from the heat and stir in the parsley. Divide the sautéed shrimp evenly among the puff pastry shells.

Whatcha Know Good?

Upon its opening in 1996, Vega brought tapas to the New Orleans area a solid decade before small plate dining became all the rage here and everywhere else. An incessant world traveler, Glen Hogh keeps his intended-for-sharing hot and cold dishes fresh and interesting with inspiration he gathers from his sojourns abroad, which he then reinterprets with Gulf seafood and regional meats and produce.

Chicken Liver Mousse: Variations for All Seasons

Chef Isaac Toups, Toups' Meatery

This versatile recipe can be adapted with other spirits and spice blends to suit the seasons: The clove and nutmeg called for here are good choices for winter. Substitute a quarter cup of Lillet Blanc for the port and the zest of a lemon for the spices for summer.

Makes about 6 cups

- 2 pounds chicken livers, rinsed
- 1 tablespoon canola oil
- 1/4 cup port
- 2 tablespoons bourbon
- 2 tablespoons sugar
- Pinch of clove
- 1/4 teaspoon freshly grated nutmeg
- Salt and white pepper to taste
- 3 sticks unsalted butter cut into 1-inch cubes, at room temperature
- 12 ounces cream cheese, cut into 1-inch cubes, at room temperature
- Hearty bread (we like Simple Rustic Crusty Bread, *recipe p. 119*) for serving
- Cornichons (optional)
- Sliced radishes (optional)

Add the livers and the oil to a medium pan set over high heat and cook until the livers are medium rare, about one minute per side. Add the port, bourbon, sugar, clove, nutmeg, salt, and pepper. Remove the pan from the heat immediately when livers are cooked through, about four more minutes. Scrape mixture into a bowl; chill.

Add liver mixture, butter, and cream cheese to the bowl of a food processor. Pulse until completely smooth. Correct seasonings with salt and pepper.

Scrape mixture into one large or several small porcelain ramekins. Chill. Serve with bread rounds, cornichons, and sliced radishes.

Whatcha Know Good?

As screwy as it sounds cooked-to-order, real-deal Cajun cracklins were not available in New Orleans until Chef Isaac Toups and his fabulous wife Amanda opened Toups' Meatery in 2012. Hell, only a small handful of places were even serving real Cajun food. What a relief that this self-proclaimed coonass corrected this terrible travesty to make the day a bright one as Cajun culinary traditions are now alive and well in the city. The ever-entertaining, Rayne, Louisiana native never fails to impress at his eponymous meat palace. Check it for lamb neck, rillons, hog's headcheese, pimento cheese deviled eggs topped with fried chicken skin, fried boudin balls, country ham, a zillion different pickled vegetables, kicky house-made condiments, Moroccan olives, a kick-ass wine list, and killer seasonal house cocktails. Fun, fun, fun!

Smoked Des Allemands Catfish Fritters

Chef Dana Honn, Carmo Kitchen

Chef Dana Honn uses local catfish for a regional adaptation to Caribbean Bacalitos (salt cod fritters) at his popular restaurant and bar, where he serves foods inspired by cuisines found in 43 tropical countries.

If you live in or around New Orleans, you can find Des Allemands catfish at the Tuesday Crescent City Farmer's Market at Jeannie Fonseca's booth, Des Allemands Outlaw Katfish Co. Outside of the area, it is preferable to use wild-caught catfish from a clear water source.

Cassava meal can be found at Brazilian and African groceries, and will often be referred to as farina de manioca or garri.

In this recipe, the catfish is lightly cured before smoking, which slightly alters the texture of the fish. This dish must be started at least twenty-four hours before you intend to cook the fritters.

Makes about 20 fritters

1 pound wild catfish fillets, preferably Des Allemands
2/3 cup sea salt
2 large russet potatoes, peeled and cubed
3 tablespoons olive oil
2 tablespoons minced garlic
1/4 cup thinly sliced scallions
2 tablespoons chopped flat leaf parsley
1 poblano pepper, finely minced
1 finely minced Scotch Bonnet or Serrano pepper, optional
3 large eggs, well beaten
Salt to taste
Peanut oil for frying
1/2 cup of cassava meal or corn meal
Caribbean style or vinegar-based hot sauce, such as Crystal, for serving

Wash and pat dry the catfish fillets. Cover them evenly and generously with half a cup of sea salt and place them in a glass loaf dish, layering as needed. Cover with plastic wrap and apply a 1-pound weight to the top, distributing the weight as evenly as possible. A 1-pound package of beans works well for this. Refrigerate for four to six hours or overnight.

Pour off any accumulated liquid from fish. Sprinkle the remaining sea salt on the fillets and refrigerate for another six to eight hours or overnight. Again, pour off any accumulated liquid. Pat the fillets dry.

To smoke the fish, prepare an indoor stove-top smoker or an outdoor smoker as desired with a subtly flavored wood, such as pecan or alder. Smoke the fish until it is firm to the touch and flakes easily with a fork. Smoking times will depend on the device being used: A stove-top smoker could take as little as fifteen minutes on medium heat while a vertical charcoal smoker could take up to an hour or more. Cool the fish and flake it with a knife and fork.

Add the potatoes to a large pot. Cover with water and boil until tender, about fifteen minutes. Drain, cool, and mash the potatoes. Set aside.

Heat the olive oil in a sauté pan set over medium heat. Add the garlic and cook until fragrant, about two minutes. Add the reserved mashed potatoes. Remove from heat and add the flaked fish, scallions, parsley, and peppers. Stir to blend. Add the eggs and stir rapidly to blend and cool. Add salt to taste. The consistency should be thick enough that it stands up on its own, without spreading out.

Heat the oil to 380°F. in a deep fryer or Dutch oven.

Use two tablespoons to form 2-ounce elongated football-shaped portions (quenelles) about three inches long, and dust with cassava or corn meal. Working in batches, fry the quenelles until golden brown, about three minutes, turning if necessary. Remove with a slotted spoon and drain on butcher paper or paper towels. Serve with hot sauce.

Whatcha Know Good?

Des Allemands, a small community about thirty-five miles from downtown New Orleans, is situated along a bayou of the same name. Settled in 1721 by resourceful German immigrants, the area it has become known as the Catfish Capital of the Universe, due to the proliferation of wild catfish that are distinct for their small size, firm flesh, and mild flavor.

Tortilla Española (Vegetarian)

Chef Glen Hogh, Vega Tapas Café

Tortilla Española is an ideal dish for savoring during long visits with friends at the table, and it is particularly wonderful for brunch. It can be made before everyone arrives and served cut in wedges at room temperature. Blanching the potatoes before roasting them ensures a silken texture inside with a crisp outer texture.

Serves 4

- 1 large Yukon Gold potato, peeled and diced
- 5 eggs
- 2 egg whites
- 1/2 cup grated Manchego cheese
  Kosher salt and freshly ground pepper to taste
- 2 tablespoons extra-virgin Spanish olive oil
- 1/2 medium onion, finely chopped
- 1/2 cup diced bell pepper (red or a combination of red and green)
- 2 small roasted piquillo peppers from a jar, cut into slivers

Add potatoes to boiling water and cook until just tender, about five minutes. Drain and cool.

Preheat oven to 400°F.

In large mixing bowl, combine cooled potatoes, eggs, egg whites, and 1/4 cup of the cheese. Add salt and pepper and fold gently to combine. Set aside.

Heat oil in an oven-safe sauté pan over medium-high heat; add onion and sauté until just fragrant, about one minute. Add diced red pepper and sauté until onions are translucent, about two minutes more.

Reduce heat to medium and pour reserved egg and potato mixture atop sautéed vegetables. Top with strips of piquillo pepper. Cook mixture just until sides begin to bubble and brown slightly, about four minutes. Scatter remaining cheese atop. Place pan in oven and bake until golden brown and fully set, ten to twelve minutes. Cool and cut into two-inch wedges.

Whatcha Know Good?

Through its cuisine and atmosphere, Vega celebrates Southeast Louisiana's oft-forgotten Spanish culinary heritage rather than the French customs that came later and eclipsed the colony's early roots. Thick velvet drapes seal the space off from the outside bustle of Metairie Road, and sensual colors, glass mosaic tiles, a silk-draped ceiling, and abundant candlelight set the backdrop for a tapas sharing experience. At once chic and sexy, casual and easy, this Old Metairie spot has earned its ranking as a favorite destination for successful first dates.

Badass Bacon Bean Dip

Chef Neal Swidler, Juan's Flying Burrito: A Creole Taqueria

Experiment with other varieties of dried beans to change the flavor profile a bit or substitute vegetable lard for the bacon fat to make a vegan version.

Makes about 4 cups

1/2 pound of bacon
1 pound dried pinto beans, soaked overnight, drained
2 tablespoons olive oil
1 small onion, large diced
3 small green bell peppers, diced
1 tablespoon chopped garlic
1 teaspoon chili powder
1 tablespoon minced pickled jalapeño peppers
Salt to taste
Sour cream for serving
Salsa Fresca for serving (recipe follows)
Minced green onions for garnish
High-quality tortilla chips or flour tortillas for serving

Fry the bacon until crispy and drain it on paper towels. Reserve the rendered bacon grease.

Add beans to a pot, cover with two inches of water, set over high heat, and bring to a boil. Reduce heat to maintain a simmer and cook until tender, about forty-five minutes.

Meanwhile add the olive oil to a sauté pan set over medium-high heat. Add the onion, bell pepper, and garlic. Reduce heat to low and sweat mixture until onions are translucent, about ten minutes. Add the chili powder, pickled jalapeño, and salt. Set aside and keep warm.

Remove the beans from the heat. Stir and allow to rest. After resting, the remaining cooking liquid should just barely cover the beans. If more remains, drain it off. Blend in the reserved onion mixture. Set aside.

Heat 1/2 cup of the reserved bacon drippings over high heat in a large pot or Dutch oven. Use a sieve to drain half of the beans over the pot holding the beans. Add the drained beans to the pot with the rendered fat. Cook, stirring steadily as the beans dissolve into the hot fat, about five minutes. Pour the bacon drippings and bean mixture into the pot containing the reserved beans and liquid. Use an immersion blender to process the beans until nearly smooth but still retaining some texture. Scrape into one large or several small serving bowls. Top with sour cream, Salsa Fresca, green onions, and reserved crumbled bacon. Serve with chips or warm tortillas.

Salsa Fresca

Makes about 5 cups

3 medium vine-ripened tomatoes, preferably Creole, finely chopped
1 medium onion, finely chopped
2 cloves garlic, minced
1 tablespoon olive oil
1 tablespoon freshly squeezed lime juice
Chili powder to taste
2 tablespoons chopped fresh cilantro
Sea salt to taste

Combine tomatoes, onion, garlic, olive oil, lime juice, chili powder, cilantro, and salt in a large glass bowl. Refrigerate for at least one hour.

Whatcha Know Good?

According to Warren Chapoton, founder and president, Juan's Flying Burrito "lit up" on a really funky stretch of Lower Magazine Street on Feb.7, 1997, just before Mardi Gras. If the trippy menu, tatted staff, and fun-house-meets-punker-music-club environment are any indication they've been lightin' up ever since. Loosely based on the San Francisco Mission style burrito joints that were hot in the 80's and early 90's, Juan's differentiated itself with Creole-laced, kinda-sorta Tex-Mex-ish food to order and finished a la minute on the grill. Devoted to local food culture and value pricing, Juan's expanded to offer its Hecho en NOLA with a second spot in Mid City in 2002. This is a place I will never tire of: A truly wacky New Orleans style Mexican joint with creative interpretations of traditional dishes from both cultures. Hang on tight for Mardi Gras Indian tacos, Hawaii 5-0-4 nachos, Bacon Azul quesadillas and top shelf margaritas that will make your head spin.

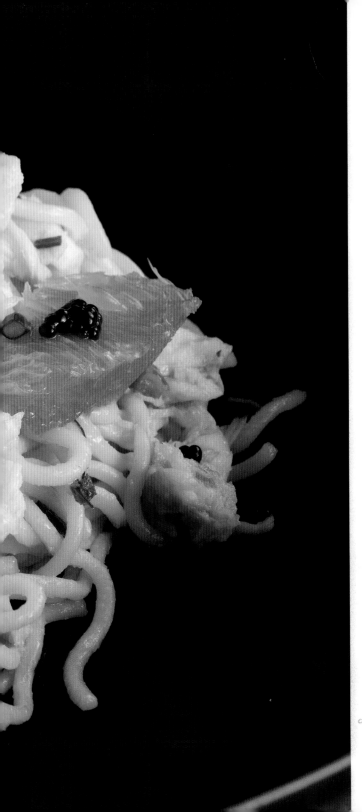

Chilled Crab and Cappellini Salad

Chef Isaac Toups, Toups' Meatery

With bright flavors and brilliant colors, this super-easy-but-elegant pasta salad is an excellent choice for holiday entertaining when citrus is at its prime.

Serves 4

    Juice of 1 lemon
1 tablespoon Dijon mustard
1 teaspoon sugar
2 tablespoons extra-virgin olive oil
    Salt and white pepper to taste
8 ounces dried cappellini pasta cooked until *al dente*, chilled
1 tablespoon chopped fresh parsley
1 tablespoon chopped fresh chives
1 ounce of your favorite caviar
8 ounces jumbo lump Gulf crabmeat, picked over for shells and cartilage
20 satsuma, tangerine, or blood orange segments, membranes removed
4 large basil leaves, cut in a chiffonade

Start with well-chilled ingredients.

Whisk the lemon juice, mustard, and sugar in a bowl until the sugar has dissolved. Add the oil in thin rivulets, whisking constantly until emulsified. Season with salt and pepper.

Add the cappellini, parsley, chives, and caviar; toss gently to coat.

Gently fold in the crabmeat, taking care not to break up the lumps.

Divide the salad evenly among four chilled salad plates. Divide the citrus segments and basil evenly among the plates.

Whatcha Know Good?

The Plaquemines Parish citrus crop, regarded by many as the finest of its kind in the world (Harry & David use the fruit for their exclusive culinary mail-order business), has been decimated again and again by freezes and hurricanes, as much of the parish is situated on a finger reaching into the Gulf of Mexico. It is a testament to the tenacity of the people of Plaquemines, devoted as they are to their way of life and unwilling to accept defeat, that they have rebuilt their land, replanted their crops, and wrested their harvests from the land over and over. The fruits of their labor are, indeed, superior products: Autumn brings fat satsumas that tantalize the tongue, grapefruits and Moro oranges with flesh the color of persimmon juice, syrup-sweet navel oranges, and Meyer lemons with heady aromas that offer a hint of the rich juices they hold. As the months turn colder, Louisiana sweet oranges, tangelos, mandarins, and kumquats brighten the dreary winter like bursts of sunshine.

Market Vegetable Salad with Cashew Purée, Black Olive Praline, and Citrus Vinaigrette (Vegan)

Chef Michael Stolzfus, Coquette

This utterly beautiful, highly textured salad makes the very best of fresh, seasonal produce and can easily be adapted to satisfy vegan, raw, and traditional diets. Each component of this guest-worthy showstopper should be prepared in advance and the salad assembled at the last moment. Enjoy the applause.

Serves 6

10 varieties colorful seasonal vegetables (such as tiny broccoli or cauliflower florets, radishes, carrots, peas, asparagus, beets, tomatoes), shaved or cut into bite-sized pieces (may use fresh or pickled varieties or a combination)
Citrus Vinaigrette *(recipe follows)*
Cashew Purée *(recipe p. 119)*
Assorted soft herbs such as chervil, dill, or chives, torn and/or stemmed as necessary
Black Olive Praline *(recipe p. 119)*, crumbled

If using fresh vegetables, blanch or leave raw as desired. Chill.

Toss the vegetables in the Citrus Vinaigrette.

Spread the Cashew Purée evenly among six chilled salad plates. Divide the vegetable mixture among each of the plates. Garnish with the herbs and crumbled Black Olive Praline.

Citrus Vinaigrette

Makes 3/4 cup

1/4 cup fresh orange juice
1/4 cup fresh grapefruit juice
  2 tablespoons seasoned rice wine vinegar
1/4 cup extra-virgin olive oil
     Sea salt to taste

In a large bowl, combine orange juice, grapefruit juice, and vinegar. Gradually stream in the olive oil in thin rivulets, whisking constantly until emulsified. Season with sea salt. Chill.

Pickled Watermelon and Shrimp Salad with Ginger-Lime Vinaigrette

Sam Hanna, Hanna's Kitchen

Sweet, cold, zesty, and lightly salty with brilliant colors: This is an easy, impressive do-ahead choice for summer entertaining.

Serves 4

- 1/4 cup sugar
- 1 tablespoon fresh tarragon or 1 1/2 teaspoons dried
- 1/2 cup red wine vinegar
- 1/2 cup tarragon vinegar
- 1 thick slice seedless watermelon, rind discarded, cut into 1-inch squares
- 1 cup mesclun greens
- 12 jumbo domestic shrimp, peeled, deveined, boiled, and halved horizontally
  Ginger-Lime Vinaigrette (recipe follows)
  Shredded carrot for garnish

Combine the sugar, tarragon, and vinegars in a sauce pot set over medium-high heat. Simmer for fifteen minutes. Remove from heat, strain, and cool.

Submerge the watermelon in the liquid. Refrigerate for at least ten minutes. Drain watermelon.

Divide the mesclun among four chilled salad plates. Divide shrimp and watermelon cubes evenly among the plates. Drizzle each with Ginger-Lime Vinaigrette and garnish with shredded carrots. Serve ice cold.

Ginger-Lime Vinaigrette

Makes 1 1/2 cups

- 1 cup rice wine vinegar
- 2 tablespoons sugar
- 2 teaspoons minced pickled ginger
- 1/2 teaspoon red pepper flakes
- 4 tablespoons lime juice
- 1/2 cup vegetable oil
  Salt to taste

Combine the vinegar, sugar, ginger, and pepper flakes in mixing bowl. Whisk until sugar is dissolved. Whisk in lime juice. Gradually stream in the oil in thin rivulets, whisking constantly until emulsified. Add salt. Set aside in refrigerator to chill.

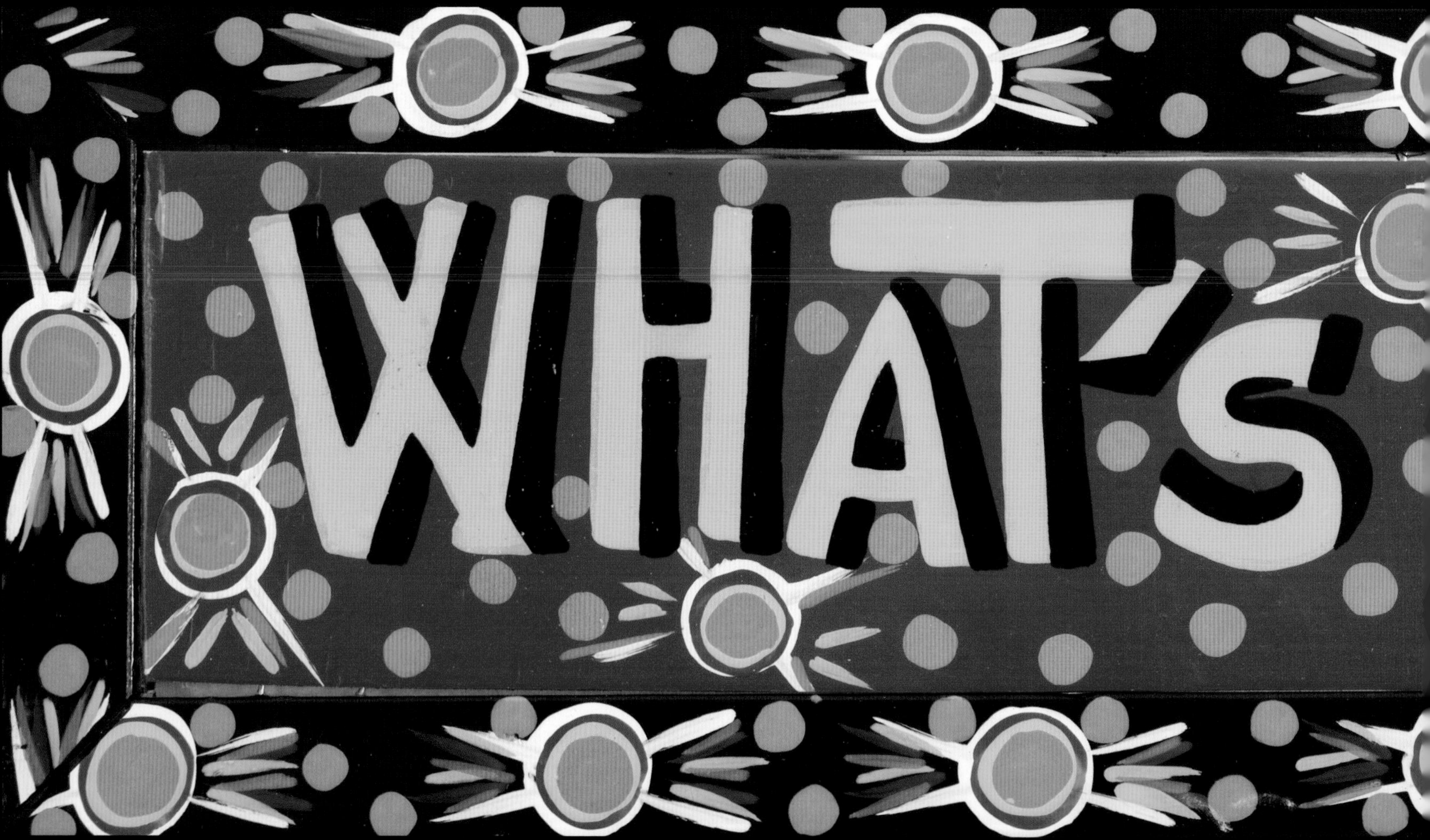
WHAT'S

COOKIN'

SIMON 2014

Land & Air

Grilled Short Ribs with Charred Mustards and Louisiana Shallots

Chef Michael Gulotta, MoPho

Ask your butcher to cut the short ribs across the bone in pieces one and a half inches thick. Short ribs cut this way are readily available in Asian and Latin markets. Louisiana shallots are green onions with large white bulbs. They are also called spring onions and are available in farmer's markets.

Com Dep is a dried rice cereal available in Asian markets. Unsweetened crispy rice cereal could be substituted.

Serves 6

3 pounds bone-in short ribs
   Short Rib Marinade *(recipe p. 120)*
   Canola oil
   Salt to taste
2 cups Short Rib Glaze *(recipe p. 120)*
2 bunches mustard greens, washed, thicker stems removed
1 bunch Louisiana shallots, rinsed, and split in half lengthwise
2 cups Ginger Vinaigrette *(recipe p. 120)*
2 limes, cut in quarters
   Freshly ground black pepper
   Fresh leaves of mint and cilantro, picked
   Edible flowers for garnish, if desired
1 cup Com Dep (see note above) tossed with 1 heaping tablespoon smoked paprika (pimenton de la vera), optional

Put the short ribs in a zip-top plastic bag. Pour in the marinade. Refrigerate overnight.

Rub the marinated ribs with oil and sprinkle evenly with salt. Place the ribs on a grill or grill pan over medium heat and slowly cook for about twenty minutes, flipping the ribs every five minutes or so. Brush the ribs with the Short Rib Glaze, increase the heat to high, and grill for another five minutes, flipping the ribs halfway through and brushing with more glaze. Set aside.

Place the mustard greens and shallots on the grill or in the grill pan. Cook the mustard greens until wilted and lightly charred, about thirty seconds. Remove the greens and set aside. Continue cooking the shallots until they are charred and tender, about four minutes more.

Heap the mustard greens on a serving platter and drizzle liberally with Ginger Vinaigrette. Place short ribs atop the greens and top the ribs with more glaze. Finish the dish with the grilled shallots, a squeeze of lime juice, pepper, cilantro and mint leaves, and seasoned Com Dep if desired.

Grilled Stuffed Quail with Pancetta

Chef Ian Schnoebelen, Mariza

To serve this for a dinner party, start two days out: Marinate the quail for one day. Then stuff it up to one day before your gathering and refrigerate until a half hour before you are ready to grill it to allow it to come to room temperature.

Serves 4

- 3 tablespoons local honey
- 3 tablespoons best-quality balsamic vinegar plus additional for serving
- 4 semi-boneless quails, cut in half vertically
  Pancetta Stuffing (recipe follows), chilled
- 8 thin slices pancetta
  Leaves from 1 head of butter lettuce, washed and dried
- 2 teaspoons olive oil, plus additional for serving
  Sea salt to taste
- 1/4 red onion, thinly sliced

Whisk together honey and balsamic vinegar. Pour the mixture into a large zip-top plastic bag. Add the quail and refrigerate for twenty-four hours.

Drain the quail and discard the marinade. Pat the quail dry with paper towels.

Spoon 1 teaspoon of the stuffing onto the inside of each breast. Fold the thigh over the breast to form a neat package. Wrap each package in a piece of pancetta.

Prepare a charcoal or gas grill for direct heat cooking. Cook the quail to desired doneness, about seven minutes in all for medium, turning every couple of minutes. Alternatively, heat a grill pan over high heat and sear the quail, turning as necessary.

While the quail is cooking, brush the lettuce lightly with olive oil and sprinkle with sea salt. Add the lettuce to the grill and cook until wilted, about thirty seconds.

To serve, divide the lettuce among four plates. Top the lettuce with the quail. Scatter the onions evenly atop the quail. Drizzle each portion lightly with additional balsamic vinegar and olive oil.

Pancetta Stuffing

Makes about 1/2 cup

- 3 ounces (about 6 tablespoons) small-diced pancetta
- 1/4 red onion, finely diced
- 1 teaspoon minced garlic
- 3/4 tablespoon chopped fresh sage
  Pinch of black pepper

Render the pancetta in a skillet over medium heat until it starts to caramelize. Add the red onion and garlic and cook until the onion is translucent, about two minutes. Add the sage and pepper. Drain to remove access fat. Chill in the refrigerator.

Scottie's CNN Blackberry and Jalapeño Ribs

Chef Scot Craig, Katie's Restaurant & Bar

Though Scottie uses this divine sauce to baste the succulent, tender ribs he serves at his Mid City restaurant, it would work equally well on chicken, pork, duck, or vegetables. "Hell, use it on tofu. But whatever you do, don't use this on those horrible, fatty St. Louis-style ribs," the chef warns. "They suck. Use only lean baby backs."

Serves 4

- 2 racks best-quality baby back pork ribs
- 1 cup ketchup
- 1 cup honey
- 1/4 cup molasses
- 1/8 tablespoons ground ginger
- 1/8 tablespoons cinnamon
- 1/4 tablespoons pepper
- 1/8 tablespoon salt
- 1 cup loosely packed brown sugar
- 20 fresh blackberries
- 30 pickled jalapeño slices, finely chopped
  Pickled juice from jalapeños
  Fresh, whole blackberries, if desired

Smoke the ribs as desired for three to four hours until tender. Refrigerate the ribs until well chilled.

Combine the ketchup, honey, molasses, ginger, cinnamon, pepper, salt, sugar, blackberries, and jalapeño in a saucepot. Purée with an immersion blender. Set pot over medium heat and cook, stirring frequently, until sauce thickens, about ten minutes. If sauce gets too thick, it may be thinned with some of the pickled juice from the jalapeños.

Prepare an outdoor charcoal or gas grill for indirect cooking. Brush the ribs generously with the sauce and grill until heated through. The sauce should be thick enough to stick to the ribs.

Serve the ribs with additional sauce and blackberries, if desired.

Whatcha Know Good?

Back in 2005, with New Orleans nearly empty, vandals and thieves seized upon Katie's Restaurant just hours before the levees failed following Hurricane Katrina, flooding the popular neighborhood joint with six feet of filthy, greasy, gasoline-laced water. Scot Craig was left with neither a business, nor, since he lived upstairs, a home.

"But still, Katrina is the best thing that ever happened to me. It changed my life."

Days after the disaster, a friend encountered a group of CNN journalists seeking a mobile kitchen so they could get away from the military-issued, vacuum-sealed meals ready to eat (MREs) they were subsisting on. The friend connected the journalists and Scottie.

"I was desperate and I sensed this was a killer opportunity. I found them a mobile kitchen and they got me along with the deal. I was gonna stick like glue."

Scottie and his mobile kitchen set up shop at the CNN outpost in a parking lot not far from Lee Circle. In those early days only military, journalists (which now included Scottie), and crafty, connected types capable of securing passes were allowed to roam the city. Inexplicably, those with high-level connections included Arthur J. Robinson, aka Mr. Okra, the city's best-known traveling produce salesman. Regardless that he was awakening to a sparsely populated, utterly decimated place, back in those dark days Mr. Okra cheerily continued to do the same thing he'd done each morning for decades: He loaded up his pick-up truck with fresh fruits and vegetables and slowly drove around town singing out through a bullhorn what items he had available for sale.

"I have no idea where he was getting this stuff—most people were still munching MREs and jars of pickles—but every day it was 'I've got blackberries!' when Mr. Okra drove by. He seemed to have blackberries just coming out of his a--. So I bought blackberries.

"CNN headquarters kept sending in loads of baby back ribs. So I had lots of ribs and lots of blackberries. What to do? This is it.

"I was supposed to work for CNN for three months, tops. I ended up working for them until 2007. They changed my life. I love those guys. I still get calls from CNN bureaus all over the country asking for these ribs."

Lamb Sliders with Creole Tomato Chutney

Chef Daniel Esses, The Three Muses

With an assertive dose of fresh herbs suspended within the pork and lamb mixture, these little burgers plump up into succulent little morsels. The piquant Tomato Chutney is a hugely flavorful counterpoint and the zesty pickle chips make everything zing.

Serves 6

1 1/2   pounds ground lamb
1/2   pound ground pork
1   small onion, finely diced
5   cloves garlic, minced
1/2   cup flat-leaf parsley, chopped
1/2   cup cilantro, chopped
1/4   cup mint, chopped
1   teaspoon ground cumin
1/2   teaspoon red chili flakes
  Salt and freshly ground pepper to taste
4   ounces chèvre cheese blended with 1 teaspoon each minced fresh parsley, basil, and rosemary
6   slider-sized burger buns
  Creole Tomato Chutney *(recipe follows)*
  Esses' Kosher Dills *(recipe p. 120)*, sliced into sandwich chips

Heat a gas or charcoal grill for direct cooking.

Combine the lamb, pork, onion, garlic, parsley, cilantro, mint, cumin, chili flakes, salt, and pepper in a large mixing bowl and blend thoroughly. Form the mixture into six even patties.

Grill to desired doneness, about five minutes per side for medium.

To serve, top the bottom half of each bun with the burgers. Spread the top halves of the buns with generous layers of chèvre. Serve with Creole Tomato Chutney.

Whatcha Know Good?

Three Muses was opened in August 2010 by a trio that included Chef Daniel Esses and musician Sophie Lee. Of all the hotspots to open in post-Katrina New Orleans, Three Muses does the most comprehensive job of capturing the city's food, music, and cocktail cultures in one hip, happenin' spot. Located on Frenchmen Street in the heart of the city's local music scene, it's not just a restaurant with great music or a music club with great food or a cocktail bar with great food and music. It's all of those at the same time, cementing its place in both the city's dining and music scenes.

Creole Tomato Chutney

The composition of garam masala differs regionally, with wide variety across India. Some common ingredients are black and white peppercorns, cloves, malabar leaves, long pepper, black cumin, cumin seeds, cinnamon, black, brown, and green cardamom, nutmeg, star anise, and coriander seeds. Patak's is a reliable, readily available brand.

Makes 2 cups

1/2   cup olive oil
1   small onion, diced
3   cloves garlic, minced
1   tablespoon garam masala paste (see above)
2   cups chopped ripe tomatoes, preferably Creole, or 1 (14.5-ounce) can chopped tomatoes
2   tablespoons sugar
1/4   cup red wine vinegar
  Salt and freshly ground pepper to taste

Heat the oil in a saucepan set over medium heat. Add the onion. Cook until translucent, about five minutes. Add the garlic and garam masala. Mix well and cook for one minute or until paste has melted and blended with other ingredients. Add the tomatoes and stir. Reduce the heat to low and cook for fifteen minutes or until the tomatoes break down. Add the sugar and vinegar. Purée with an immersion blender or food processor.

Cast-Iron Chicken Fricassee with Creamy Stone-Ground Grits and Braised Collards

Chefs Keith and Nealy Frentz, Lola, Covington

Chicken Fricassee is an easy, soul-warming dish to come home to after a long day. To make it in a slow cooker, reduce the amount of stock used to 1 quart (4 cups) and add the sautéed vegetables and browned chicken to the cooker with the garlic, thyme, salt, pepper, Worcestershire, tomato paste, wine, and stock at once. Place the lid and set it to cook for four (high), six (medium), or eight (low) hours. The chicken will be falling from the bones when you walk in the door.

The greens can be cooked the night before and the grits come together quickly. Instant Southern dinner party!

Serves 6

1/2 cup canola oil	1 bay leaf
1 chicken, cut into 8 pieces	2 teaspoons dried thyme
Creole seasoning	Salt and pepper to taste
1 cup all-purpose flour	1 teaspoon Lea & Perrin's Worcestershire
3 ribs celery, diced	2 tablespoons tomato paste
1 yellow onion, diced	2 cups white wine
2 green bell peppers, diced	2 quarts chicken stock
1 carrot, peeled and diced	Creamy Stone-Ground Grits (recipe p. 121)
4 cloves garlic, minced	Braised Collard Greens (recipe p. 121)

Preheat the over to 375°F.

Heat the oil in a large pot or Dutch oven, preferably cast iron, set over medium-high heat. Season the chicken with the Creole seasoning and dredge it in the flour. Reserve excess flour. When the oil is hot, add the chicken and brown on both sides. Set aside.

Add the reserved flour to the existing oil and drippings in the pan to make a medium-dark roux, stirring constantly, about fifteen minutes. Add the celery, onion, bell pepper, and carrot, and sauté until the onions are translucent, about ten minutes. Scrape the bottom of the pot to loosen the fond. Add the garlic, bay leaf, thyme, salt, pepper, and Worcestershire and cook until fragrant, about four minutes. Add the tomato paste, wine, and stock and stir till thick. Continue cooking until the sauce is thick enough to coat the back of a wooden spoon, about twenty minutes. Add the chicken to the pot and cover. Put the pot in the oven and cook until chicken is tender and cooked through, about one hour. Serve with Creamy Stone-Ground Grits and Braised Collard Greens.

Chicken-Fried Sweetbreads with Lamb Sausage Gravy and Pickled Mustard Greens

Chef Jeremy Wolgamott, High Hat Café

If veal sweetbreads are unavailable, skinless dark chicken could be substituted for a similar effect.

Serves 6

2	pounds veal sweetbreads
1	quart buttermilk
4	cups all-purpose flour
1	cup coarse cornmeal
1	tablespoon kosher salt
1	tablespoon black pepper
1/4	teaspoon cayenne
	Oil for frying
	Lamb Sausage Gravy (recipe p. 121)
	Pickled Mustard Greens (recipe p. 122)

Use a paring knife to remove the veins from the sweetbreads. Break the sweetbreads into roughly 2-ounce pieces and add them to a bowl with the buttermilk. Set aside.

Combine the flour, cornmeal, salt, and peppers. Set aside.

Using a skillet or deep fryer, heat the oil to 350°F.

Remove the sweetbreads from the buttermilk and dredge each in the seasoned flour. Working in batches, fry the sweetbreads until they are golden and reach an internal temperature of 165°F., about five minutes, turning if necessary. Drain on paper towels.

Divide the gravy among six bowls. Divide the sweetbreads among the bowls and garnish each with a spoonful of the pickled greens.

Pork Trotter Gumbo with Deviled Eggs

Chef Michael Stolzfus, Coquette

Historically a common ingredient in soul food cooking, the use of pig's feet in mainstream cuisine has become more widespread since the financial crisis of the late-2000s, when chefs and home cooks discovered the luxurious texture obtained when the dirt-cheap trotters cook slowly in stock and release their rich gelatin.

Could there possibly be a more Southern combination than pig foot gumbo served bobbing with deviled eggs?

Trotter gumbo is one of many variations on the native roux stew served at Coquette. Chef Stolzfus recommends substituting any braised or roasted leftover meat for the trotters for variety. Additionally, any substantial greens such as beet, turnip, rapini, or dandelion greens may be substituted for the collards and mustards called for here.

"If okra is your thing, feel free to add that too. But either way, add greens to your gumbo, 'cause they're awesome."

Serves 8 to 10

- 2 cups plus 2 tablespoons vegetable oil
- 3 cups all-purpose flour
- 2 cups bacon, cubed (Chef Stolzfus likes Benton's)
- 2 cups cubed andouille sausage (Chef Stolzfus likes Jacob's brand from LaPlace)
- 2 yellow onions, diced (about 4 cups)
- 2 1/2 green bell peppers, diced (about 2 cups)
- 4 celery ribs, diced (about 2 cups)
- 3 garlic cloves, minced
- 1 teaspoon cayenne pepper
- 1 tablespoon paprika
- 1 teaspoon ground coriander
- 1 teaspoon celery salt
- 1 tablespoon onion powder
- 1 tablespoon granulated garlic
- 1 tablespoon Coleman's mustard powder (or ground yellow mustard seeds)
- 1 tablespoon picked thyme leaves
- 1 tablespoon ground black pepper
- Reserved meat and cooking liquid from Braised Pork Trotters (recipe p. 122)
- 5 or so shakes of Worcestershire sauce
- 1/2 cup Crystal hot sauce plus additional for serving
- 1 bouquet garni (a variety of mixed fresh herbs, tied with cheesecloth or butcher's twine—Chef Stolzfus uses sage, oregano, parsley, and lemon thyme)
- Salt to taste
- 2 bunches collard greens, washed, stems removed, torn
- 1 bunch mustard greens, washed, stems removed, torn
- Water or chicken stock as needed
- Hot cooked rice and Deviled Eggs (recipe p. 122) for serving

Heat 2 cups of the vegetable oil over medium heat in a cast-iron sauté pan. Slowly add the flour, whisking vigorously yet carefully to avoid being splashed with "Cajun napalm." Continue cooking, stirring constantly, until the roux is a uniform very dark brown, about one hour. You will use half of this amount. Reserve the remainder in a covered jar at room temperature for another use. This step may be done in advance. Set aside.

Add the remaining 2 tablespoons of vegetable oil to a large stockpot or Dutch oven, preferably cast iron, set over medium-low heat. Add the bacon and chopped andouille and cook, stirring occasionally, until the bacon is fully rendered and lightly crisp. Using a slotted spoon, remove the bacon and the andouille from the pot, leaving the rendered fat behind. Reserve the bacon and the andouille.

Add the onion, peppers, celery, garlic, and all the spices. Cook on low heat until the vegetables are soft and the onions are translucent, about twenty minutes. Add the roux (half of what you made) and continue cooking until the mass begins to swell and bubble. Add the reserved bacon, andouille, trotter meat, and cooking liquid, Worcestershire, hot sauce, bouquet garni, and salt to taste. Bring to a simmer, and cook, stirring occasionally, for two hours. Add additional water or stock as needed.

Add the collard and mustard greens. Stir thoroughly to incorporate, cover, remove from heat, and cool completely. Refrigerate overnight to allow flavors to marry.

Reheat, adding additional water or stock as needed to achieve your desired consistency, and correct seasoning. Serve the gumbo over rice and top with a deviled egg. Offer additional hot sauce at the table.

Grilled Ribeyes with Crab-Boil Garlic Potatoes with Swiss Chard and Maitre d' Butter

Chef Ryan Hughes, Purloo

A Southern spin on the classic Midwestern meat and potatoes pairing.

The potato and chard component of this dish may easily be served as a flavorful vegetarian or vegan entrée: If preparing a vegan version, use a vegan butter substitute when making the Maître d' Butter.

Serves 6

Vegetable oil
6 10-to-12-ounce bone-in rib-eyes or 8-ounce boneless, at room temperature
Kosher salt and freshly ground pepper
Crab-Boil Garlic Potatoes with Swiss Chard (recipe follows)
Maître d' Butter (recipe follows), chilled, cut into 1/2-inch slices

Rub the grill grate of a gas or charcoal grill with a clean dish towel or rag dipped in vegetable oil. Prepare the grill for direct heat cooking, about 500°F. Alternatively, heat a grill pan over high heat.

Season the steaks with salt and pepper. Grill steaks to desired doneness, 135°F. for medium-rare. Allow the steaks to rest for five minutes.

Divide the Crab-Boil Garlic Potatoes with Swiss Chard among six warmed dinner plates. Plate the steaks atop. Top each with a slice of Maître d' Butter.

Whatcha Know Good?

For years, Chef Ryan Hughes hosted weekly pop-up gatherings employing French culinary techniques to explore culinary traditions from across the South—from Caribbean tropical flavors to South Carolina's Low Country to Louisiana's Cajun culture. In September 2014, Purloo finally and fittingly found a permanent home in the new Southern Food & Beverage Museum on Oretha Castle Haley Boulevard in Central City.

Crab-Boil Garlic Potatoes with Swiss Chard (Vegetarian)

Serves 6

2 pounds red-skinned or new potatoes, scrubbed
1 tablespoon kosher salt
1 tablespoon liquid crab boil
3 garlic cloves, smashed
Maître d' Butter (recipe follows), chilled, cut into 1/2-inch slices
2 bunches Swiss chard or kale rinsed, dried, trimmed of ribs, torn into large pieces
1 tablespoon distilled white vinegar

Put the potatoes, salt, crab boil, and garlic in a medium saucepan, add cold water to cover by about one inch. Bring to a boil, lower the heat, and simmer until potatoes are fork-tender, about eight to ten minutes. Drain; discard the garlic. Set aside.

Heat a large sauté pan over medium heat. Melt in 2 tablespoons of the Maître d' Butter. Add the chard and sauté until just wilted, two to three minutes, stirring often. Add the vinegar and the reserved potatoes; toss gently to combine. Remove from heat and distribute evenly among six warmed plates.

Maître d' Butter

Makes 1 cup

2 sticks (1 cup) unsalted butter softened (use vegan "butter" for a non dairy version)
2 tablespoons cracked black peppercorns
2 tablespoons diced shallot
2 anchovy fillets
1 teaspoon dry mustard
1 tablespoon Worcestershire
3 tablespoons, chopped fresh parsley

In a food processor combine the butter, peppercorns, shallots, anchovies, dry mustard, and Worcestershire. Purée until uniform and smooth. Fold in the chopped parsley. Scrape the butter onto a piece of parchment paper. Roll the paper and twist the ends to form a log. Refrigerate until solid, at least thirty minutes.

Naked Veal with Fried Oysters and Preserved Lemon Aioli

Chef Greg Sonnier, Kingfish

The aioli may be made ahead of time, refrigerated and brought to room temperature as the veal is cooking.

Serves 4

- 1 egg
- 1/8 cup chopped preserved lemon *(recipe p. 123 or use store-bought from a Middle Eastern market)*
- 1/4 cup Meyer lemon juice
- 2 toes garlic, peeled
- 1 teaspoon Dijon mustard
- 1 teaspoon chopped fresh parsley
- 2 1/4 cups extra-virgin olive oil
- Salt and pepper to taste
- 4 well-pounded 3-ounce veal cutlets
- 1/4 cup flour
- Vegetable oil for frying
- 4 large Gulf oysters
- 1/2 cup yellow corn flour seasoned with Creole seasoning

To a food processor add the egg, chopped preserved lemon, lemon juice, garlic, mustard and parsley; process to combine. With the processor running, add 1 3/4 cups of the olive oil in a thin stream until fully emulsified. Season with salt and pepper. Set aside to a cool, not cold, place.

Heat the remaining olive oil in a large skillet over high heat. Season the flour with salt and pepper and gently coat the veal with the mixture. When the oil shimmers, add the veal cutlets and sear on both sides for 40 to 60 seconds. Remove the cutlets from the pan and discard the oil. Set the veal aside and keep warm.

Add the vegetable oil to the skillet over medium-high heat. When the oil is hot enough for a fleck of flour to sizzle, dredge the oysters in the seasoned corn flour and add them to the pan. Fry the oysters until golden brown, turning as necessary. Drain on paper towels.

To serve, top each veal cutlet with a fried oyster. Top each oyster with a dollop of the aioli.

Bad Bart's Black Jambalaya

Crescent Plate

It was a bold move when Bart Bell and Jeff Baron opened Crescent Pie & Sausage Company on a Katrina-wrecked stretch of Banks Street back in 2009. Wildly popular for its menu of rustic house-smoked meats and sausages served in a unique space crafted of salvaged woods, offset by unexpected bursts of bold color, the restaurant had the look of an architect-designed tree-house and crowds packed the place up until the very end in August 2014, when Bell & Baron announced they were closing the moneymaker that sits at the center of a now-flourishing neighborhood.

"When we started Crescent Pie & Sausage the area was pretty desolate," Baron said. "Tulane Avenue is experiencing the same kind of situation. We want to put all our focus and energy there. We want to put our motor behind that."

Seems like these brave restaurateurs/urban revivalists just can't help themselves. Their new spot, Crescent Plate, is an easy-on-the-wallet meat-and-three lunch spot offering four proteins and nine sides including the house-made sausages and this unique jambalaya they kept on the menu from their place on Banks Street.

Serves 12

- 1/4 cup vegetable oil
- 1 pound smoked sausage, preferably Louisiana-style, sliced into wedges
- 3 ribs celery, diced small
- 2 poblano peppers, diced small
- 1 yellow onion, diced small
- 1/2 pound braised pork
- 1/2 pound boneless and skinless roasted chicken thigh meat
- 1 12-ounce can of black-eyed peas
- 4 1/4 cups stock (chicken, pork, or beef)
- 2 tablespoons chopped fresh oregano
- 2 tablespoons chopped fresh parsley
- 2 tablespoons chopped fresh thyme
- 1 tablespoon kosher salt
- 1 teaspoon freshly ground black pepper
- 1 teaspoon granulated garlic
- 1 teaspoon cayenne pepper
- 2 cups parboiled rice

Add the vegetable oil to a four-gallon saucepan set over medium heat. Add the sausage and cook until it sizzles and curls. Add the celery, peppers, and onions and cook until golden brown, about ten minutes. Then add the braised pork and cook fifteen minutes, stirring frequently (every couple of minutes).

Add the chicken, stir, and cook for another ten minutes. Add the black-eyed peas and cook another ten minutes. Add the stock, bring to a simmer and stir in the fresh herbs, salt, black pepper, garlic, and cayenne pepper. Add the rice, bring to simmer, cover, reduce the heat to low, and cook until the rice is soft. Start checking frequently after fifteen minutes to ensure the rice does not burn.

Whatcha Know Good?

Chef Bart Bell is hardly the first to evolve the hearty rice dish we associate with Cajun (brown-style) and Creole (red-hued due to added tomato) cooking.

The New Orleans Times featured an article on June 28, 1872, where jambalaya was first mentioned. The story tells of "those who brought victuals, such as gumbo, jambalaya, etc.," and they "all began eating and drinking." The first recipe for jambalaya in a New Orleans cookbook was in Lafcadio Hearn's La Cuisine Creole in 1885, where he wrote of "jambalaya of fowls and rice," which he believed was of American Indian origin. Madame Begué certified her recipe for "jambalaya of rice and shrimps" in 1900; and the Picayune's Creole Cook Book of 1901 has recipes for jambalayas of crab and shrimp, a Creole jambalaya, as well as "au Congri" (with ham, onions, and cowpeas), and a "French Pilou." Célestine Eustis, born in Paris of New Orleans' parents, included a Jumballaya a la Creole and a St. Domingo congris in her Cooking in Old Creole Days (1904).

Fried Brussels Sprouts with Pepper Jelly Glaze (Vegan)

Chef Michael Nirenberg, Fulton Alley

Remember when Brussels sprouts were verboten? Those Dark Days when Mother had to threaten you with loss of liberty if you did not eat the wretched things she had boiled to death, stinking up the house and making you dread the dinner table?

Those days are gone. In our modern era, the lowly Brussels sprout has risen to meteoric, chic heights to become one of the darlings of the veg world, thanks to inventive chefs and cooks who figured out how to prepare them to dazzle. In this fun and breezy recipe, Chef Michael Nirenberg marries the cutie cruciferous bundles to a sweet and tangy Southern favorite. This would be as at home at a picnic as it would be on the holiday table. It can sit out for hours and still maintain its integrity.

Serves 4

   Oil for frying
1 pound Brussels sprouts, each cut in half through the core
   Salt and pepper to taste
1 cup Pepper Jelly Glaze (recipe follows) or 1 jar store-bought pepper jelly, heated and thinned with a bit of cider or chili vinegar

Heat the oil to 350°F. in a deep fryer or heavy pot. Add the Brussels sprouts and cook until golden brown, about three minutes. Drain on paper towels and season with salt and pepper. Add the Brussels sprouts and Pepper Jelly Glaze to a large bowl and toss to coat. Serve hot or at room temperature.

Pepper Jelly Glaze

This recipe is going to make more than you will need for Brussels sprouts. Use the remainder to glaze roasted poultry or meat or kick it old school and just dump some over a block of cream cheese and have at it with some good wheat crackers.

Makes 1 quart

1   red bell pepper
2   jalapeño peppers
4   Anaheim peppers
1   cup apple cider vinegar
1   cup apple juice
1/4 package of liquid pectin
1/2 teaspoon salt
3   cups sugar

Purée all peppers, the vinegar, and the apple juice. Allow to sit for a few hours or overnight to let the flavors develop. Pour mixture into a large sauce pot or Dutch oven and add the pectin and salt. Bring to a boil over medium heat. Add the sugar and return to a boil. Skim all foam that rises to the surface, then pour into a heat-proof container and allow to cool completely. Process for sealing in jars.

Mac'N on Magazine

Chef David Gotter, GG's Dine-O-Rama

Chef Gotter offers variations—what he likes to call "fancy pants mac dishes"—to this basic, though unabashedly decadent creation that proudly includes Velveeta cheese.

For a Southern-style dish, as shown here, he recommends adding 4 strips of crumbled, cooked Netsuke bacon and 4 ounces sliced, drained pickled jalapeños when you blend in the cheese. Serve the dish topped with a sliced boneless fried chicken breast.

For a Tex-Mex style presentation, he recommends skipping the truffle oil in the topping and serving the macaroni as a base topped with either pulled pork or a sliced grilled chicken breast, black beans, diced tomatoes, fresh corn kernels, sliced pickled jalapeños, and a dollop of sour cream.

Serves 4

1 pound elbow macaroni
Rich Blended Cheese Velouté (recipe follows)
Truffled Bread Crumbs (recipe follows)
Shaved Parmesan cheese

Cook the macaroni until al dente, according to package instructions. Drain. Combine the pasta and the cheese sauce in a large bowl. Divide the mixture among four serving bowls. Top each portion with a tablespoon of Truffled Bread Crumbs and a scattering of Parmesan.

Whatcha Know Good?

A psychiatrist might be able to explain how the combination of cheese and noodles taps into some happy child part of the brain. The ultimate universal comfort food has enjoyed a resurgence in popularity seemingly everywhere, but in Southeast Louisiana it never fell out of favor. We pretty much regard this sacred goo as a vegetable, and it's a sacrilege to imagine a holiday dinner without a bubbling casserole full of it sitting on the sideboard.

Rich Blended Cheese Velouté

Makes 6 cups

4 tablespoons salted butter
4 tablespoons all-purpose flour
4 cups whole milk, chilled
10 ounces Velveeta cheese, cut into 1-inch cubes
4 ounces shredded cheese blend (mozzarella, Jack, provolone, Asiago)
2 ounces mascarpone
2 ounces chèvre cheese

Melt the butter in large pan over medium heat and whisk in flour to make a blond roux. This will take about two minutes. Slowly whisk in the cold milk. Reduce heat to low and simmer, stirring occasionally, until mixture thickens, about ten minutes. Working in batches, add all cheeses, stirring constantly until cheeses melt and mixture is heated through.

Truffled Bread Crumbs

Makes 1/2 cup

2 tablespoons unsalted butter
1/2 cup panko bread crumbs
1 tablespoon white truffle oil
Salt to taste

Melt the butter in a small skillet over low heat. Fold in the bread crumbs and cook, stirring constantly, until golden and toasted, about five minutes. Remove the pan from the heat. Stir in the truffle oil and season with salt.

Tina Dunbar's Kitchen Sink Gumbo

Celestine Dunbar, Dunbar's Soul Food

Tina Dunbar learned to cook what she calls "kitchen sink gumbo" as a six-year-old perched upon a step stool her father set before the family's old stove in Paulina, La. "Mama wouldn't cook on Sundays because she spent all day at church. Daddy had to have his gumbo, so he said, 'I'll teach my little girl to make it.'"

This rich bayou stew is crowded with poultry pieces and gizzards, sausage—she declares Vernon's brand from Vacherie to be the very best—and both fresh and dried shrimp. "The dried shrimp are for flavor only. They make the flavor much more intense. I add them early on. Before they're added, the gumbo smells just like any other stew. When the dried shrimp hit, it really starts to smell good and gumbo-ish."

Serves 8 as an entrée, 16 as a soup course

- 15 chicken wings, each cut into 3 pieces at joints
- 10 cups water
- 1 cup vegetable oil
- 1 cup all-purpose flour
- 1 large onion, medium dice
- 2 bunches green onions, chopped
- 3 stalks celery, chopped
- 2 1.5-ounce bags dried Gulf shrimp
- 3 dried bay leaves
- 2 generous tablespoons dried parsley
- 2 teaspoons dried thyme
- 2 tablespoons Creole seasoning, such as Zatarain's or Tony Chachere's
- 1 tablespoon salt
- 1 tablespoon black pepper
- 2 tablespoons Kitchen Bouquet
- 1 pound chicken gizzards (optional)
- 2 1/2 pounds smoked sausage, sliced
- 1/2 pound andouille sausage or other heavily smoked pork sausage, sliced
- 2 pounds raw Gulf crabs, rinsed, cleaned, broken apart (frozen are fine)
- 3 tablespoons filé powder, divided, plus additional for serving
- 1 1/2 pounds raw medium Gulf shrimp, peeled
  Hot cooked white rice
  Louisiana-style hot sauce

Preheat oven to 350°F.

Place chicken wings on a rack set over a baking sheet. Place in oven and cook until light golden, about twenty minutes.

Meanwhile, bring water to a boil in a large stockpot. While waiting for water to boil, heat oil in a large skillet, preferably cast iron, until oil shimmers. Slowly incorporate the flour, stirring constantly, over medium high heat. Continue cooking and stirring until the roux is mahogany in color, about fifteen to twenty minutes.

Carefully spoon the roux into the boiling water, whisking constantly. Add the chicken wings, onion, green onions, celery, dried Gulf shrimp, bay leaves, parsley, thyme, Creole seasoning, salt, pepper, Kitchen Bouquet, chicken gizzards, sausage, crabs, and 1 tablespoon filé powder. Return to a boil. Reduce heat and simmer, uncovered, one hour. Add the remaining filé powder and the fresh shrimp. Cover and simmer until shrimp are just pink, about ten minutes.

Serve over rice. Offer additional filé powder and hot sauce at the table.

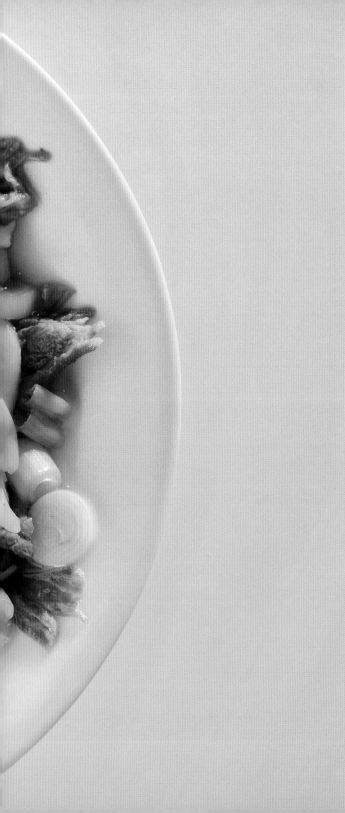

Miss Linda's Original New Orleans Ya-Ka-Mein

Miss Linda the Ya-Ka-Mein Lady/Miss Linda's New Orleans Soul Food

Ya-Ka-Mein is a combination of beef or roast pork and/or shrimp, hard-boiled eggs, green onions, noodles, and occasionally vegetables in a spicy, salty broth with heavy doses of soy sauce and black pepper. Black southern soldiers fighting abroad in the Korean War were first exposed to a version of the soup, which they consumed after a day on the battlefield or an evening in a bar to sober up and fortify themselves. They brought the tradition home with them, and it has been served in some New Orleans African American bars ever since. Often referred to as "Old Sober," devotees of the potent dish swear by its ability to alleviate the misery of a hangover.

Serves 4

- 2 quarts low-sodium beef stock
- 1 tablespoon Creole seasoning
- 1 tablespoon coarsely ground black pepper
- 1/2 cup low-sodium soy sauce plus additional for serving
- 1 pound cooked, room temperature, spaghetti
- 1 pound beef chuck roast, boiled and finely chopped, at room temperature
- 1/2 pound small boiled, peeled shrimp, at room temperature
- 2 bunches green onions, chopped
- 4 eggs, hard boiled, peeled, and halved
- Hot sauce for serving

Bring stock, Creole seasoning, pepper, and soy sauce to a boil in a large heavy-bottomed pot. Cover, reduce heat to low, and simmer ten minutes.

Divide spaghetti evenly among eight large soup bowls. Distribute chopped beef, shrimp, and green onions evenly among bowls and top each with half an egg, yolk side up. Ladle one cup of hot broth into each bowl and finish with a generous dash of soy sauce. Serve with more soy sauce and hot sauce.

NOTE: Miss Linda recommends adding blanched vegetables such as cauliflower, broccoli, and/or carrots for a heartier Ya-Ka-Mein or eliminating the meat and preparing the base with vegetable broth for a vegetarian version.

Whatcha Know Good?

For years, Shirley Green cooked Ya-Ka-Mein at Bear Brothers Bar in New Orleans' Central City neighborhood. In the early 1990s, her daughter Linda (aka Miss Linda, the Ya-Ka-Mein Lady), a former Orleans Parish Public School cafeteria cook, carried on the tradition through her eponymous catering service and started selling it from the back of her pickup truck at second line parades and from a booth at the New Orleans Jazz & Heritage Festival. Today Miss Linda's name is synonymous with her increasingly famous elixir, which is repudiated to have restorative powers.

"Not feeling well?" she'll ask. "'That's all right, Baby. What you need is a Ya-Ka-Mein right now to make you feel better.'"

Smothered Okra and Charred Tomatoes (Vegan)

Chef Michael Doyle, Maurepas Foods

Both shiso and lemon balm are herbs used in Asian cooking and both are related to mint. They are available in the produce section of Asian markets.

Served hot or cold, this fresh, vibrant blend is ideal as a vegan meal served over rice or as an enhancement to meat, poultry, or fish. If serving this dish as a main course, cut the okra into three-quarter-inch sections for a heartier version.

Makes about 4 cups

- 5 large, fresh, ripe tomatoes, preferably Creole, halved
- 4 sprigs shiso (may substitute 4 large basil leaves and 15 small mint leaves)
- 2 cups loosely packed lemon balm leaves
- 2 tablespoons vegetable oil
- 2 medium onions, diced
- 2 1/2 pounds fresh okra, sliced to 1/4-inch pieces
- Salt
- Sriracha sauce to taste

Set the oven broiler to high and position an oven rack about four inches below it. Arrange the tomatoes on a rimmed baking sheet and broil until the tomatoes are heavily charred on one side, about fifteen minutes. Turn the tomatoes and put a heavy char on the other side as well. Let cool.

Scrape the tomatoes and any juices into a bowl. Add the shiso and lemon balm leaves to the tomatoes and purée with a blender, immersion blender, or food processor. Set aside.

Add the oil to a covered Dutch oven set over medium-high heat. Add the onions and cook until translucent, about five minutes. Add the okra, reduce the heat to medium-low, cover, and sweat the mixture, stirring occasionally, until the okra begins to soften, about fifteen minutes. Add the tomato mixture and cook until thickened and reduced, about fifteen minutes. Season with salt and Sriracha. Serve hot or cold.

Whatcha know good?

In early 2012, Chef Michael Doyle led the charge in making the Bywater neighborhood a hip dining destination when he evolved a former corner printing house into a lovely, window-lined restaurant and bar. Casual, affordable, and outfitted with reclaimed wood and Warholian-esque art, the space is as energetic and idiosyncratic as the neighborhood it's set in. Most of the farm-fresh goods used to create the minimalist cuisine and inventive cocktails are grown just for the restaurant and harvested at Pelican Produce in the nearby Upper Ninth Ward.

Summer Squash Ratatouille (Vegan)

Chef Scot Craig, Katie's Restaurant & Bar

An easy vegan side dish, Chef Scottie created this summery blend as part of a meal he cooked for President Bill Clinton after he adopted a no-meat-no-dairy lifestyle to stave off mounting health problems.

Serves 4

- 2 medium yellow crookneck squash, unpeeled
- 2 zucchini, unpeeled
- 2 tablespoons olive oil
- 1/2 red or yellow onion, thinly sliced
- 1/2 each red and green bell peppers, thinly sliced
- 4 ounces sliced button mushrooms
- 2 cloves garlic, minced
- 2 teaspoons minced fresh thyme leaves or 1 teaspoon dried
  Creole seasoning

Cut the yellow squash and the zucchini in half lengthwise, then slice the lengths into quarter-inch discs. Set aside.

Heat the olive oil in a large skillet over medium-high heat. Add the onion and cook until translucent, about four minutes. Add the reserved squash, zucchini, bell peppers, and the mushrooms, garlic, and thyme. Cook until squash just begins to soften but still retains some snap, about five minutes. Season with Creole seasoning.

Whatcha Know Good?

"So, in 2013 right before Jazz Fest, I get this kinda panicky phone call from my friend (New Orleans resident and political analyst) James Carville. 'So Scottie, can you come cook dinner for me and some friends tomorrow night? One of 'em's vegan. Can you cook vegan?'

"Sure, why not."

"So I'm setting up in the kitchen making vegan dishes alongside the crawfish étouffée and shrimp Creole James just loves and in walks Bill Clinton. Instead of heading right in to talk to all of his famous friends—and the house was loaded with them—he comes in the kitchen and starts chatting with us. He's asking me about my restaurant, asked how we made out back in the Katrina days. He told us that at 67 he was the oldest living man in his family due to heart disease, so he's taken up a vegan lifestyle. He was so gracious I half expected him to start doing dishes.

"Then, a couple of weeks later, you know what I get? A thank-you note. The former President of the United States sent me a hand-written thank-you note for cooking him dinner and giving him a Katie's T-shirt. What a nice guy. This one's for him."

Toups' Double-Cut Pork Chop with Dirty Rice and Cane Syrup Gastrique

Chef Isaac Toups, Toups' Meatery

Put the pork chops in the brine at least twenty-four hours—and up to two days—before you cook them. Do not skip the brining process: It changes the texture and flavor of the meat and lends a sweet, juicy quality.

The sweet and tart flavors of the Gastrique cut beautifully through the richness of the pork and the assertive flavors in the Dirty Rice. This would be a grand slam for a special dinner gathering.

Serves 4 to 6

1/2 gallon water
1 cup dark brown sugar, loosely packed
1 cup kosher salt
2 bay leaves
   Ice
4 double-cut pork chops, frenched
   Salt and pepper to taste
   Dirty Rice (recipe follows)
   Cane Syrup Gastrique (recipe p. 123)
   Diced green onion, for garnish

Combine the water, brown sugar, salt, and bay leaves. Bring to a boil in a large sauce pot. Add ice until the volume reaches 1 1/2 gallons. Pour the brine into a container large enough to hold it and the pork chops. A small ice chest works well. Add the pork chops and refrigerate for twenty-four to forty-eight hours.

Preheat the oven to 400°F.

Remove the pork chops from the brine, pat dry with paper towels, and liberally salt and pepper both sides of the chops.

Place a large grill pan over high heat. Leave undisturbed until smoking. Add the pork chops and sear heavily on both sides. Place the pan in the oven and cook until it reaches an internal temperate of 145°F. Allow to rest five minutes before serving.

To serve, place a generous scoop of Dirty Rice on each of four plates. Top with pork chops. Spoon the Gastrique generously atop the chops. Garnish with diced green onion.

Whatcha Know Good?

After ten years in Chef Emeril Lagasse's kitchens, in 2012 Chef Isaac Toups and his wife, Amanda, opened Toups' Meatery to showcase their considerable collective gifts. Isaac's kitchen mastery, his Cajun family's deep centuries-old relationships with the land, and Amanda's vast knowledge of wine acquired through years of management and education as a French wine scholar are a formidable combination.

Dirty Rice

Chef Toups' Maw Maw Cart gave up the secret to her addictive Dirty Rice: It's the cumin that makes it really shine.

Makes about 8 cups

2 tablespoons vegetable oil
2 1/2 tablespoons all-purpose flour
1/2 pound ground beef brisket
1/2 pound ground pork
   Salt to taste
1 teaspoon cumin
1 teaspoon black pepper
1 teaspoon paprika
1 teaspoon cayenne
3/4 cup chicken stock
3 cloves garlic, crushed
3 cups cooked white rice (Chef Toups likes Jazzmen brand)
1 tablespoon unsalted butter

Add the oil to a heavy Dutch oven, preferably cast iron, set over high heat. Add the flour and stir vigorously with a wooden spoon or wire whisk until a dark roux is achieved, taking extreme care not to burn. Scrape the roux into a bowl. Set aside.

Wipe out the Dutch oven with paper towels.

Combine the ground brisket and pork in a large bowl and blend thoroughly. Add the salt, cumin, pepper, paprika, and cayenne. Heat the Dutch oven, over medium-high heat. Add the seasoned meat and cook until it is brown and the fat has rendered out, about ten minutes. Continue cooking until a fond (brown bits) develops on the bottom of Dutch oven. Deglaze with a half-cup of chicken stock, taking care to scrape up all of the fond. Add the crushed garlic and reserved roux and continue cooking for twenty minutes, adding the remaining chicken stock as needed to keep meat mixture from drying out.

Add the rice and butter; combine thoroughly.

Sea

Cream of Blue Crab and Wild Mushroom Bisque

Chefs Keith and Nealy Frentz, Lola, Covington

Fortunate culinarians have a source from which to gather wild mushrooms—there are several spots in the woods on the north shore of Lake Pontchartrain—and the smarts to know which ones are suitable for consumption. If wild mushrooms are unavailable, dried ones reconstituted in hot water may be used. Save the water in which they soak to enrich broths and stocks.

Serves 8 as an entrée, 16 as a soup course

- 2 sticks plus 3 tablespoons salted butter
- 4 ribs celery, medium dice
- 1 onion, medium dice
- 2 green bell peppers, medium dice
  Salt and freshly ground pepper to taste
- 4 cloves garlic, minced
- 2 cups all-purpose flour
- 2 bay leaves
- 2 teaspoons dried thyme
- 4 tablespoons Crystal hot sauce
- 2 cups dry white wine
- 2 cups heavy cream
- 3 quarts crab or seafood stock
- 3 pounds fresh, wild mushrooms such as chanterelle, chicken of the woods, porcini, oyster, or shitake or 9 ounces dried, reconstituted in hot water
- 1 pound jumbo lump Gulf crabmeat, picked over for shells and cartilage

Melt 2 sticks butter in a large, heavy pot over medium heat. Add the celery, onion, bell pepper, salt, and pepper. Sauté until the vegetables are soft, about ten minutes. Add the garlic. Stir in the flour, blending thoroughly. Cook, stirring constantly, until a light blonde roux is achieved, four to five minutes.

Add the bay leaf, thyme, hot sauce, wine, and stock, whisking constantly to incorporate. Add the cream and whisk to incorporate. Cook over medium-low heat until mixture starts to thicken, about twenty minutes. Remove the bay leaves and purée the mixture using an immersion blender. Set one-fourth of the mushrooms aside; add remainder to the puréed soup and cook until mushrooms are tender, ten to fifteen minutes. Adjust seasoning.

Meanwhile, add remaining three tablespoons butter to a skillet set over medium high heat. Add remaining mushrooms and sauté until golden, about ten minutes. Set aside.

Turn off fire under soup; gently stir in crabmeat. Allow to sit until crab is heated through. Serve each portion garnished with some of the sautéed mushrooms.

Whatcha Know Good?

Working within in the cramped confines of their vintage railroad caboose turned kitchen, married Chefs Keith and Nealy Frentz turn out as many as 555 dishes each day for lunch alone, rarely exchanging more words than the obligatory warning "behind you," when one is passing the other's rear with a hot pot. Theirs is a mutual devotion to producing studied examples of fine contemporary Southern cuisine with farm fresh local ingredients and Gulf seafood. Rarely is one in the downtown Covington kitchen without the other and there are never more than two people present at a time. Occasional help is provided by a lone kitchen employee. They will close the restaurant for the day rather than open without at least one of them present.

Though both chefs are multi-disciplined, Nealy gravitates naturally toward baking and Keith finds his place at the stove. Their diminutive forty-seat restaurant presents by day in rustic elegance with warm, aged wood and stained glass. The space is transformed with candlelight, flowers, and twinkling crystal glasses on Friday and Saturday evenings, the only nights they're open.

Shrimp and Tasso Tacos with Pickled Okra and Pepper Jelly

Nate Kelly, Juan's Flying Burrito: A Creole Taqueria

Nate Kelly, general manager of Juan's Mid City, came up with the idea for this playful riff on the famed Shrimp Henican from swanky Commander's Palace. This kind of creativity is a signature at Juan's: Many of their people, including Nate, joined the staff after defecting from the likes of Commander's, Restaurant August, and Emeril's.

Makes 6 tacos

18 medium Gulf shrimp, peeled and deveined
 1 teaspoon Creole seasoning
 1 teaspoon minced garlic
 1 tablespoons olive oil
 6 ounces tasso, diced small
 2 tablespoons Salsa Fresca (recipe p. 33)
 6 6-inch flour tortillas
 1 cup finely shredded red and/or green cabbage
 3 tablespoons pepper jelly, warm
 6 whole pickled okra pods, split lengthwise
   Sliced green onions, for garnish

Combine the shrimp, Creole seasoning, garlic, and olive oil in a medium bowl. Allow to marinate for twenty to thirty minutes before cooking.

Preheat oven to 300°F.

Heat a heavy skillet, preferably cast iron, over high heat. Add the shrimp and tasso and sear, turning as necessary until shrimp are just pink and the fat begins to render from the tasso, about three minutes. Add the Salsa Fresca and cook until the shrimp are fully pink, two to three minutes. Set aside.

Warm the tortillas in the oven for four to five minutes.

To serve, divide the shrimp and tasso evenly among the tortillas. Top each with cabbage, then drizzle with a half tablespoon warm pepper jelly and two okra spears. Garnish with green onions, if desired.

BBQ Shrimp Gaufre

Chef Greg Sonnier, Kingfish

This unexpected sweet-savory brunch entrée marries two of Louisiana's best-known indigenous ingredients and would be an excellent way to kick off a festive holiday morning: Use large, best-quality store-bought waffles, make the sweet potato mixture the night before, and reheat. The shrimp cook in minutes.

Serves 4

- 2 pounds sweet potatoes, peeled, cut into 1-inch cubes
- 1 tablespoon vegetable oil
- Zest and juice of 2 oranges
- 1/2 cup light brown sugar, loosely packed
- Pinch of ground cloves
- 1 teaspoon vanilla extract
- 1 teaspoon cinnamon
- Pinch of salt
- 6 tablespoons chilled, unsalted butter
- 1 teaspoon cracked black pepper
- 1 teaspoon finely chopped rosemary

- 16 jumbo shrimp (about 2 pounds), peeled in center, heads and tails intact
- 2 teaspoons Creole seasoning
- 1 tablespoon finely chopped garlic
- 4 5-inch round or oblong waffles
- 1 tablespoons Worcestershire sauce
- 1/4 cup Abita beer
- 1/2 cup seafood stock
- Juice of 2 lemons
- 4 sprigs fresh rosemary for garnish

Preheat oven to 350°F.

Toss the potatoes with the vegetable oil. Spread on a baking sheet, place in the oven, and roast until the potatoes are tender, about twenty minutes. Keep oven warm.

Add the potatoes to the bowl of a food processor with the orange zest and juice, brown sugar, clove, vanilla, cinnamon, and salt. Purée until smooth. Keep warm until ready to serve.

Add 2 tablespoons butter to a skillet set over medium heat. When the butter has melted, add the pepper, rosemary, and shrimp. Increase heat to high. Add the Creole seasoning and garlic; sauté until the shrimp are pink, about four minutes.

Place the waffles in the oven to warm.

Add the Worcestershire, beer, and stock; bring to a boil and allow liquid to reduce by half, about five minutes. Add the lemon juice; return to a boil and immediately remove the pan from the heat; blend in the remaining chilled butter, stirring until emulsified.

Spread the top of each of the warm waffles generously with the warm sweet potato mixture; divide the shrimp evenly atop each. Spoon the pan sauce atop the shrimp and around the waffles. Garnish each with a sprig of fresh rosemary.

Whatcha Know Good?

Kingfish can be a tough reservation to land with many weekend nights selling out months in advance since its 2013 opening. The irresistible combination here is kitchen wizard Greg Sonnier manning the stove; old-school veteran bartender Chris McMillian pouring stiff, classic New Orleans libations; and a wait staff comprising a cast of chatty characters who found their way here after lives first lived in other realms—one of them as a Pulitzer prize winning journalist, for example.

It all comes together as a strangely appropriate tribute to Huey P. Long, the Kingfish himself, whose likeness and memorabilia adorn the French Quarter space.

Crawfish Beignets

Chef Scot Craig, Katie's Restaurant & Bar

Like many over-the-top delicious foods, Chef Craig's riff on the Jazzfest Crawfish Bread he loves so much came to him late one night when he was "starving and kinda drunk."

This recipe has been altered to accommodate the home cook while protecting just a couple of the chef's coveted secrets. If you have access to fresh pizza dough—either because you make your own or you have a pizzeria willing to share—by all means use it.

Serves 4 as an appetizer

> Oil for frying
> 12 ounces fresh pizza dough
> (or use 1 13.8-ounce roll store-bought dough, such as Pillsbury Classic Pizza crust)
> 8 ounces Cheddar cheese, shredded
> 8 ounces provolone cheese, shredded
> 1 cup Caramelized Onions (recipe follows)
> 16 pickled jalapeño slices (optional)
> 8 ounces Louisiana crawfish tails with fat
> Zesty Aioli (recipe follows)

Add oil to a deep fryer. Preheat to 350°F.

Roll out dough on a lightly floured surface; divide into four equal portions. Shape each portion roughly into a circle.

Layer the cheeses, caramelized onions, jalapeño slices, and crawfish tails evenly among the four circles. Fold each circle in half to form a crescent (like a mini calzone). Crimp edges tightly so ingredients will not leak.

Cook each beignet in hot oil until golden, about seven minutes, turning as necessary. Drain on paper towels.

Serve with Zesty Aioli.

Caramelized Onions

Additional onions may be stored in an air-tight container in the refrigerator for up to three days or frozen for up to one month.

Makes about 2 cups

> 5 large onions, sliced into strips, not rings
> 5 tablespoons olive oil
> Salt to taste
> 1 teaspoons sugar (optional)
> 1/4 cup balsamic vinegar (optional)

Use a wide, thick-bottomed sauté pan, ideally cast iron, for maximum pan contact with the onions. Coat the bottom of the pan with olive oil and set over medium-high heat until the oil is shimmering. Add the onions and stir to coat. Spread the onions evenly over the pan and cook, stirring occasionally, for ten minutes. Reduce the heat if you feel you are losing control of the cooking process. Add a little water if you feel they are drying out.

After ten minutes, sprinkle salt and optional sugar over the onions. If the onions start sticking to the pan, let them stick a little and brown, but then stir them before they burn. After the first twenty to thirty minutes, you may want to lower the stove temperature and/or add a bit more oil if the onions are verging on burning. Scrape the browned bits from the pan as you stir. You will have to scrape more as you progress.

Continue to cook and scrape, cook and scrape, until the onions are a rich mahogany color, about one hour in all. Deglaze the pan with the vinegar, if desired, scraping the browned bits and stirring back into the onions.

Zesty Aioli

Ideally, make the Zesty Aioli the night before and refrigerate to allow the flavors to marry.

Makes about 1 cup

> 1 cup best-quality mayonnaise
> 1 teaspoon minced roasted red pepper
> 1 teaspoon minced pickled jalapeño pepper
> Pickled jalapeño juice from the jar

Combine mayonnaise, roasted pepper, and jalapeño. Thin with jalapeño juice as necessary to achieve pourable sauce.

Juan's Shrimp with Cheddar Grits and Chipotle Butter

Chef Adam Sandroni, Juan's Flying Burrito: A Creole Taqueria

New Orleans' much-beloved, truly funky Creole Taqueria puts a Southwestern spin on a Southern brunch classic. Sop up the delicious sauce with torn bits of warm tortilla.

Serves 4

- 16 jumbo Gulf shrimp, peeled and deveined
- 1/2 teaspoon ground cumin
- Creole seasoning to taste
- 2 tablespoons vegetable oil
- 1/2 cup Salsa Fresca *(recipe p. 33)*
- 1/2 cup white wine
- 1 cup Chipotle Compound Butter, melted (recipe follows)
- Cheddar Grits (recipe follows)
- Fresh chopped cilantro and spears of fried tortillas for garnish, optional
- Warm flour tortillas for serving

Season the shrimp with the cumin and Creole seasoning.

Add the oil to a large sauté pan set over medium-high heat. Add the shrimp and the Salsa Fresca and cook until shrimp are pink, about five minutes. Deglaze the pan with the white wine and scrape the bits from the bottom of the pan.

To serve, divide the Cheddar Grits among four shallow bowls or plates. Divide the shrimp evenly among the plates. Drizzle with melted Chipotle Compound Butter and garnish with chopped cilantro and tortilla spears. Serve with warm tortillas.

Chipotle Compound Butter

This is also adds zippity do dah to corn, grilled meat, and hot cornbread.

Makes about 1 cup

- 1 cup (2 sticks) salted butter softened
- 1/4 cup finely chopped fresh cilantro
- 1/4 cup finely chopped fresh flat-leaf parsley
- 1 tablespoons finely minced garlic
- 1 finely minced chipotle chile in adobo sauce (from a can)
- 2 tablespoons adobo sauce (from a can)

Combine butter, cilantro, parsley, garlic, chile, and adobo sauce in a bowl and use a spatula to blend thoroughly. Scrape the mixture onto a length of parchment paper and twist the ends to form a log. Refrigerate or freeze until ready to use.

Cheddar Grits

Makes about 4 cups

- 5 tablespoons unsalted butter
- 1 cup fresh corn kernels scraped from the cob
- 3 cups water
- 3 cups milk
- Salt
- 1 teaspoon white pepper
- 1 teaspoon granulated garlic
- 1 1/2 cups stone-ground grits
- 3/4 cup extra-sharp shredded Cheddar cheese

Add 1 tablespoon butter to a small skillet over medium-high heat. Add the corn kernels and sauté until softened, about five minutes. Set aside.

Combine remaining butter, water, milk, salt, pepper, and garlic in a sauce pot or Dutch oven; bring to a boil. Reduce the heat to low, add the grits, and cook until liquid has absorbed, twenty to thirty minutes. Stir in corn and cheese and cook until heated through and cheese is melted, about two minutes.

Trout Baquet

Chef Wayne Baquet, Li'l Dizzy's Café

A food vendor for the Jazz & Heritage Festival since the annual gathering's first days, Wayne Baquet turns out thousands of portions of his family's eponymous Gulf fish dish to satisfy his adoring public. The goal here is to get a crisp golden buttery line along the edge of the fish and take extreme care to keep the lumps of crabmeat whole. Together you have the perfect bite.

Serves 6

6 6-ounce fillets of speckled trout (may substitute drum)
　Creole seasoning
　All-purpose flour for dusting
8 tablespoons unsalted butter, divided
6 cloves of garlic, peeled and minced
1 tablespoon fresh lemon juice
1 pound jumbo lump crabmeat—picked for cartilage and shells
　Chopped parsley and lemon wedges for garnish

Season the fish with Creole seasoning on both sides and very lightly dust with flour. Add 4 tablespoons of the butter to a flat-top griddle or a hot well-seasoned cast-iron skillet. Add fish and sear on both sides until golden, about two minutes per side. Set the fish aside and keep warm.

In a separate sauté pan over medium heat, melt the remaining butter and add the lemon juice and the garlic. Once the garlic is softened, add the crabmeat. Cook until just heated through, two to three minutes. Adjust seasoning as necessary. To serve, gently spoon hot sauce over cooked fish, sprinkle with parsley, and serve with lemon wedges.

Whatcha Know Good?

It is not in the new, daring, or innovative that Wayne Baquet distinguishes L'il Dizzy's, his Creole Soul food restaurant at the corner of Esplanade Avenue and North Robertson in Treme. The lifelong restaurateur/chef makes his mark with simple classics like buttery Trout Baquet and seafood-stuffed folded omelets prepared to perfection, as well as labor-intensive Creole heritage dishes like Crawfish Bisque that increasingly few are willing to fool with.

Oyster and Cauliflower Gratin with Country Ham

Chef Jeremy Wolgamott, High Hat Café

The unexpected marriage of oysters and cauliflower prepared in the manner of a classic casserole typify the daring approach contemporary Louisiana chefs are taking to evolve the region's native cuisines while still keeping their foods identifiable as being of the South.

Serves 6

4 cups diced stale French bread
2 cups diced or shaved Manchego cheese
1 bunch fresh parsley, stemmed
1 head cauliflower, heart removed, florets roughly chopped into bite-size pieces
1/2 stick (1/4 cup) unsalted butter
1 yellow onion, diced small
Pinch of crushed red pepper
1/4 cup all-purpose flour
2 cloves garlic, minced

2 cups whole milk
1 cup heavy cream
Juice of 1 lemon
1 teaspoon hot sauce (Chef Wolgamott likes LA brand)
Salt and pepper to taste
1/2 pound thinly sliced country ham, cut in a chiffonade (Chef Wolgamott likes Broadbent's brand)
36 shucked Gulf oysters

Preheat the oven to 400°F.

Combine the bread, cheese, and parsley in a food processor and process until fully pulverized. Set aside.

Place the cauliflower florets on a baking sheet and roast them in the oven until they just begin to color, about ten minutes.

Meanwhile, melt the butter in a heavy pot or Dutch oven set over high heat. Add the onions and sweat them down until they are translucent, about five minutes. Add the roasted cauliflower and crushed red pepper and cook, stirring constantly, until the cauliflower starts to caramelize, about eight minutes. Add the flour, stirring constantly until fully incorporated, about one minute. Add the garlic and cook until fragrant, about 2 minutes. Pour in the milk and cream and bring to a boil, stirring constantly. Reduce the heat to a simmer and season with lemon juice, hot sauce, and salt and pepper. Cook the mixture until it is thick and the floury taste is gone.

Increase the oven temperature to 450°F.

Spread a layer of the bread crumb mixture across the bottom of a greased 9 x 13-inch glass dish or six greased individual gratin dishes. Add a layer of the country ham, then a layer of raw oysters, then a layer of the cauliflower mixture, then another layer of the bread crumb mixture. Bake until the bread crumbs are turning golden brown and the sauce is bubbling rapidly, about five minutes for individual gratins and as long as fifteen minutes for a casserole dish.

Whatcha Know Good?

Open since 2010, High Hat Café still has the ambiance and brings about the comforting feelings of a favorite meat-and-three diner that's been in the neighborhood for years, yet it eschews the notion that an everyday joint must serve the same old thing. The food here intersects the cooking of the Mississippi Delta with that of New Orleans.

Seared Flounder with Artichoke and Green Olive Giardiniera

Chef Ryan Hughes, Purloo

Chef Ryan Hughes' hybrid of the classic oil-rich Italian olive salad we find in our familiar muffalettas and the pickled vegetables of giardiniera makes a pungent topping for the sweet, flaky richness of sautéed flounder. It's a quick, impressive meal: Make the giardiniera in advance and bring it to room temperature. Just sear off the fish and you're good to go.

Serves 4

4 4 to 6-ounce Gulf flounder fillets, skin-on
   Salt and freshly ground pepper
4 tablespoons extra-virgin olive oil
   Artichoke and Green Olive Giardiniera (recipe follows)

Season flounder with salt and pepper. Heat olive oil in heavy-bottomed sauté pan or cast-iron skillet over high heat until just smoking. Sear flounder, skin side down, until it has cooked three-quarters of the way, about four minutes. Flip the fish (if it is stuck to the pan wait another ten seconds), and finish cooking until the fish is just opaque and flakes easily with a fork, one minute more.

Arrange 1 cup room temperature Artichoke and Green Olive Giardiniera on each plate. Top each with flounder, skin side up.

Artichoke and Green Olive Giardiniera (Vegan)

Make this vegan salad well in advance and stash it in the refrigerator so the flavors will marry. Bring it to room temperature before serving. The salad is delicious on its own or mince it up to dress a sandwich or toss it with pasta, cubed Italian cheeses, and salami, if desired, for a fast, hearty meal.

Makes about 1 quart

1 green bell pepper, large dice
1 red bell pepper, large dice
1 celery stalk, large dice
1 medium carrot, medium dice
1 small onion, finely chopped
1/2 cup salt
2 globe artichokes, trimmed, blanched and quartered, stems attached
1 cup pitted and roughly chopped green Spanish olives
2 cloves garlic, finely chopped
1 tablespoon dried oregano
1 teaspoon red pepper flakes
1/2 teaspoon black pepper
1 cup white vinegar
1 cup extra-virgin olive oil

Place green and red peppers, celery, carrots, and onion into a large bowl. Stir in salt, and add enough cold water to cover vegetables. Cover; refrigerate overnight.

Drain and rinse vegetables. In a bowl, combine artichokes, olives, garlic, oregano, red pepper flakes, and black pepper. Pour in vinegar and olive oil, and mix well. Scrape mixture into the large bowl with the vegetable mixture, cover, and refrigerate for two days before using.

Sweet

Banana Bread Pudding with Extra-Boozy Rum Sauce

Miss Linda the Ya-Ka-Mein Lady/Miss Linda's New Orleans Soul Food

Linda Green is an absolute scream, and being around her just makes you feel soooo good— like you do with your best girlfriend—even if you just met her.

In relaying this recipe, she said: "Bake until the pudding rises and it turns a nice-looking shade of brown. Girl, that's when you know you've got it going on, and it's gonna be some kind of damned good."

With an endorsement like that, who could possibly resist this up-cycle for stale bread?

Serves 10 to 12

4	cups whole milk
4	eggs
1 1/2	cups sugar
1/2	cup light brown sugar, packed
1/4	cup rum
1/2	teaspoon ground cinnamon
1/4	teaspoon ground nutmeg
1	tablespoon vanilla extract
2	mashed ripe bananas
1	loaf stale New Orleans-style French bread, torn or cut into cubes
	Rum Sauce (recipe follows)

Lightly grease a 9 x 12-inch baking dish and set aside. Preheat oven to 350°F.

Thoroughly blend the milk, eggs, sugars, rum, cinnamon, nutmeg, and vanilla with an electric mixer or an immersion blender. Fold in the mashed bananas.

Add the bread to a very large bowl; pour the milk mixture over. Use your hands to gently toss the bread cubes in the liquid, taking care not to squish up the bread. Gently scoop the bread into the baking dish. Do not press the bread down: The goal is to create a finished dish with lots of texture and plenty of little nooks and crannies of lightly crispy bread to capture the sauce when you serve the bread pudding.

Bake for forty-five to fifty minutes, until completely set and golden. Serve warm with Linda's Boozy Rum Sauce.

Extra-Boozy Rum Sauce

A bold and boozy sauce from a bold and beautiful lady.

Makes about 1 cup

1	tablespoon cornstarch
2/3	cup cold water
1/2	cup sugar
1/4	cup dark brown sugar, packed
1/2	cup dark rum
1	tablespoon salted butter
3/4	teaspoon vanilla extract

Dissolve cornstarch in the water.

In a nonreactive saucepan, bring sugars, rum, and cornstarch mixture to a boil over medium heat. Cook, stirring constantly, until sauce thickens, about ten minutes. Remove from heat. Add the butter; stir until incorporated. Mix in the vanilla. Keep sauce warm until ready to serve.

Whatcha Know Good?

It was more than twenty years ago when Linda Green started Miss Linda's Catering, specializing in New Orleans soul food, which she sold from the back of her truck along second line parade routes, and from booths at the New Orleans Jazz & Heritage Festival, the Essence Festival, and area farmer's markets.

A lifetime of hard work and long hours in the kitchen started to pay off in 2012. The former school cafeteria cook beat out three other local chefs to win the $10,000 prize and a place in the spotlight on an episode of the Food Network's Chopped: Pride of New Orleans. "When Chopped called and asked me to try out for the show, I had never heard of Chopped, so I asked my grandbaby about it. He said, 'Maw-Maw, that's a good show. You can do that. You can run with that crowd.' So I tried out. When they called and told me I was on the show, I started screaming like one of those people from The Price is Right.

"Then I went to New York and did the show. They handed us baskets of stuff and we had to cook with it. One thing that really got me was this: I can clean any fish—an eel, anything— but the one fish I don't like to mess with is catfish. So what turns up in my basket? A whole damned catfish. I am scared to death of that pointy thing they have; you touch that pointy thing and it's all over with for you. Fast as I could I grabbed a knife and whacked that pointy thing off. Then I fried his ass."

Louisiana Pecan Praline Bites

Langlois Culinary Crossroads

Amy Sins created these insanely delicious, super-easy little morsels because they stand up better to New Orleans' wicked humidity than traditional pralines. "You can get some mileage out of these," she says. "They look pretty sitting out for hours—if they last that long—and they freeze beautifully: Just bake, cool, and store in a zip-top freezer bag. Just crisp them up in the oven before serving. Voila!"

Makes about 30

	Nonstick cooking spray
1/2	cup all-purpose flour
3/4	cup melted salted butter
1	egg, well beaten
1	cup dark brown sugar, packed
1	cup chopped pecans

Pre-heat oven to 350°F.

Spray a nonstick mini muffin pan with nonstick cooking spray (yes, this is necessary).

Combine flour, butter, egg, sugar, and pecans in a mixing bowl, blending thoroughly.

Divide mixture evenly into muffin pan, filling each cavity three-quarters full.

Bake until edges of each muffin are lightly brown and crispy, about fifteen minutes.

This recipe cannot be doubled. It's just one of those weird things that must be accepted. If you need to double the recipe, make two batches.

Whatcha Know Good?

In 2012, Gonzales native Amy Cyrex Sins evolved Langlois Culinary Crossroads, her elegant hybrid cooking school/restaurant on Pauger Street in the Faubourg Marigny, out of the bones of a turn-of-the-century space that had most recently been Dave's Bar and before that Ferarra and Sons Italian Grocery.

"Food has always been my passion," Amy said. "I always wanted a career in food, but did not want to have a restaurant, because I wanted to see people eat what I cooked. I wanted to witness their 'ah-ha!' moments, but you don't get that if you are back in the kitchen cooking. So I kept on trying to figure it out."

She traveled extensively, taking many cooking classes in foreign locales following the publication of the Ruby Slippers Cookbook: Life, Culture, Family, and Food after Katrina (2006), a cookbook/memoir she wrote after her extended family lost all of their cherished recipes and for which she won the International Gourmand Cookbook Award. Her time abroad served to fully enlighten her to the rarity of what we have in Louisiana. "I grew up with our food and our culture and kind of took it all for granted, but I realized that our food is truly different than anything anywhere else in the world. That's when I figured it out: I knew I wanted to share our food and culture at home and educate people to share with others, so I created Langlois."

Celestine's Honey-Peach Pound Cake

Celestine Dunbar, Dunbar's Soul Food

The peaches may be steeped in honey up to two days before and refrigerated until use. The peaches are also delicious served atop vanilla ice cream. Or purée the mixture and use as a baste when grilling pork or poultry.

Be forewarned: Unless you are a magician, it is highly unlikely that this cake will release beautifully from the pan. It is more probable that the top will get stuck in the pan and you will have to dig it out with a spoon and slather it back on the cake. Whatever. Just cover up the foibles with a big puff of confectioners' sugar and serve it right up. It is homey, satisfying, and beautiful in all of its imperfect glory.

Makes 8 servings

- 2 cups local honey
- 1 tablespoon ground cinnamon
- 9 fresh, juicy Southern peaches, un-peeled, sliced (use 4 cups frozen peaches if fresh are out of season)
- 2 cups sugar
- 2 cups all-purpose flour
- 2 teaspoons baking powder
- 1/2 cup whole milk
- 2 sticks salted butter, at room temperature
- 1 teaspoon vanilla
- 1/2 teaspoon almond extract (optional)
- 5 large eggs
  Unflavored nonstick cooking spray
  Powdered sugar

Preheat oven to 300°F.

Heat the honey in a cast-iron pan over high heat. Add the cinnamon and boil for five minutes. Add the peaches and return to a boil. Reduce the heat and simmer until the peaches are soft, about fifteen minutes.

Meanwhile, prepare batter.

Combine the sugar, flour, and baking powder in a large bowl. Make a well in the center and add the milk, butter, vanilla, extract, and eggs. Beat on high speed with an electric mixer until smooth and thoroughly incorporated.

Spray a large Bundt pan generously with cooking spray. Pour two inches of batter across the bottom of the pan. Using a slotted spoon, add a layer of peaches atop batter. Pour an inch and a half layer of batter over the peaches to cover thoroughly. Add another layer of peaches. Finish with a thin layer of the batter to cover. Stop a half-inch from the top of the pan. Reserve remaining peaches.

Place cake pan atop a baking sheet and bake until set and light golden, about ninety minutes to two hours.

Cool cake completely, about two hours or overnight. Invert onto cake plate. Using a slotted spoon, arrange reserved peaches along circumference of cake. Carefully spoon honey syrup over cake until the cake is saturated. Dust the top of the cake with powdered sugar.

NOTE: If there is leftover cake batter, it may be used to make a small loaf cake or discard.

Whatcha Know Good?

It was 2002 when I shared a holiday meal with Celestine "Tina" Dunbar and her family in their Carrollton-area home in New Orleans. I met Tina in the mid-1990s when I became a regular patron of Dunbar's, her humble Creole/soul food restaurant on Freret Street. I loved it there. Tina was always warm and welcoming; you could eat like royalty for five dollars or less.

In 2005, flooding following Hurricane Katrina hit Tina's restaurant hard, filling it with several feet of greasy, brown muck. Zero flood insurance and limited personal resources led to the shuttering of the humble yet proud eatery. Hell-bent on re-opening, Tina forged a unique relationship with Loyola University and reopened Dunbar's in the cafeteria of the university law center's student union on the Broadway campus. She and her family opened the doors on their new operation in 2006.

I was recently reminded of that holiday I spent with the Dunbar family in their home when I heard whispers that Tina is close to signing a deal on another building of her own.

Chocolate Peanut Butter Crème Brulée

Chef David Gotter, GG's Dine-O-Rama

This over-the-top diet buster is about as decadent as they come and would be a suitably impressive ending to swanky dinner party. It also seems like a sure bet for a cheer-up during a solo pity party.

Make the custards the day before and leave them in the refrigerator. Just before serving, sprinkle them with sugar and hit them with your trusty little culinary torch. If you do not have one, consider investing. You can score one for about thirty bucks at major retail stores. Use it to put a quick, attractive browning or toasting on just about anything.

Serves 8

  11 egg yolks
  1/2 cup sugar plus additional for sprinkling
  1 quart (4 cups) heavy cream
  6 ounces dark chocolate (72 percent cocoa or higher)
  3/4 cup peanut butter
      Whipped cream and fresh berries for serving, optional

Whisk the egg yolks and the sugar together in a large stainless steel bowl until mixture is pale yellow. Set aside.

Preheat the oven to 300°F.

Add the cream to a large sauce pot set over low heat. Add the chocolate and peanut butter and cook, stirring constantly, until the mixture is fully liquid and smooth.

Temper the egg mixture by slowly adding a quarter-cup of the cream mixture, whisking constantly. Add the remainder of the cream mixture, whisking constantly. Divide the mixture among eight shallow buttered ramekins. Place the ramekins in a large baking pan. Open the oven and place the pan within. Carefully pour in enough boiling water to come half way up the sides of the ramekins. Bake the custards until set, about forty-five minutes. Remove the ramekins from the water bath and cool completely. Refrigerate for at least two hours.

To serve, dust the tops of each of the custards with about 1 teaspoon of sugar and caramelize the sugar with a propane torch. Garnish with whipped cream and berries if desired. Serve immediately.

Whatcha Know Good?

Named after a gunpowder magazine (warehouse) that was built at the western end of the street in the late eighteenth century, the lower part of Magazine Street was initially used as a storage area for commercial and industrial goods.

Each block of the narrow, rambling thoroughfare that stretches from the outskirts of the French Quarter (downtown) to the Mississippi River levee just past Audubon Park (uptown) wears a different mask—commercial, seedy, ultra hip and cool, country-cozy, cutesy, and provincial, quietly residential—and most have taken on defining shopping, dining, and nightlife venues. Located midway along the thoroughfare's five-mile stretch at the corner of Seventh Street, GG's Dine-O-Rama has the added benefit of outdoor seating for a front row view onto a showcase teaming with only-in-New Orleans characters and sites.

Fresh Watermelon Sorbet (Vegan)

Chef Ian Schnoebelen, Mariza

This simple, brilliantly hued sorbet offers a sweet, clean finish to a light summer meal. It also makes a divine float when scooped into ice-cold lemon-lime soda.

Serves 4

4 cups sugar
2 cups water
6 cups fresh, ripe watermelon cubes, rind and skin removed
  Juice of 2 limes

Add the sugar and water to a sauce pot set over high heat and bring to a boil. Remove from heat and cool.

Purée the watermelon in a blender. Combine the watermelon juice and sugar syrup in a large bowl. Whisk in the lime juice, cover, and chill overnight.

Process the mixture in an ice cream maker according to manufacturer's instructions. Alternatively, the liquid may be frozen until slushy, puréed in a blender, and re-frozen to achieve the proper consistency.

Whatcha Know Good?

Ian Schnoebelen is one of those people who showed up in New Orleans and just never left. "It was 1993 and I'd never been here before. I thought it would be a fun adventure. I had a garage sale back in California and sold everything I owned and moved to New Orleans on Amtrak with two trunks. I thought I was moving to the swamps, but I fell in love with it."

At Mariza, his second restaurant in New Orleans, he uses classic European technique to create Italianesque dishes inspired by a personal strain of refined Southern comfort food with California-fresh sensibilities. The food is as unique, precise, and as daring as Ian himself.

Pretzel Bread Pudding

Chef David Gotter, GG's Dine-O-Rama

Serves 4 to 6

11 egg yolks
1 cup sugar
1 tablespoon vanilla
1 quart heavy cream
2 loaves Pretzel Bread (recipe p. 123), cut into 1/2-inch cubes
Salted caramel ice cream, caramel sauce, chocolate sauce, and/or fresh berries for serving, optional

In a large bowl, combine the egg yolks, sugar, and vanilla and whisk until thoroughly blended and mixture is a pale yellow color. Slowly whisk in the heavy cream. Place the Pretzel Bread cubes in a greased 9 x 13-inch baking dish. Pour the egg mixture over the bread and toss lightly to ensure all bread is coated. Refrigerate for two hours.

Preheat oven to 300°F.

Cover the pan with foil and place the baking dish in a larger pan. Place the pan in the center of the oven and carefully pour enough boiling water into the pan to come halfway up the sides of the baking dish within. Bake the pudding until the center is set, about ninety minutes. Carefully remove the pans from the oven and extract the baking dish from the larger pan. Cut into squares and serve hot or cold with desired toppings.

Whatcha Know Good?

Though it's enjoyed a recent surge in popularity, pretzel bread is in no way a new concept. The traditional yeasty bread brought over from German immigrants has long been a staple in New York. The only problem is, until recently most of us knew pretzel bread only as dry, greasy soft pretzels—something to be eaten in desperation from an airport kiosk. But soft, flavorful pretzel bread, the way it's supposed to taste, is a fine thing, indeed. It was only a matter of time before a New Orleans chef would morph it into a bread pudding that somehow manages to be both dense and airy.

Bananas Foster French Toast

Surrey's Café & Juice Bar

There are lines out the door every morning—not just on weekends—at both of Greg Surrey's namesake restaurants on Magazine Street. After television food personality Guy Fieri featured this signature dish on Diners, Drive-Ins, & Dives, the lines swelled ever more.

Here's a tip: Assemble the stuffed French toast and chill overnight or for a couple of hours to set up the filling before slicing, dipping, and frying the toast. Having a firmer filling makes this utterly decadent dish much easier to work with.

Serves 4 to 6

2　eggs
2　tablespoons sugar
1　teaspoon vanilla extract
1　cup half-and-half
1　loaf New Orleans-style French bread, cut in 4 pieces
1　ripe banana, sliced into rings
　　Bananas Foster Cream (recipe follows)
　　Vegetable oil
　　Rum Sauce (recipe follows)
　　Confectioners' sugar for garnish

Whisk together eggs and sugar in a mixing bowl. Add the vanilla and continue whisking until sugar has completely dissolved. Whisk in the half-and-half. Set aside.

Slice each of the pieces of bread in half horizontally, leaving edges intact to form a hinge. Divide sliced banana evenly among open-hinged bread. Top banana slices evenly with Bananas Foster Cream. Close the hinged, stuffed bread sections. Carefully slice each section into four diagonal pieces.

Coat the bottom of a large sauté pan lightly with oil. Set pan over medium heat.

Dip each slice of bread into the reserved batter. Working in batches, add slices to pan and cook until golden, turning once, about three minutes per side.

Divide the warm sauce evenly among warm plates. Top each with stuffed bread; dust with confectioners' sugar.

Bananas Foster Cream

2　ripe bananas
1　cup dark brown sugar, packed
8　ounces cream cheese, softened
1　teaspoon vanilla extract

Add bananas, brown sugar, cream cheese, and vanilla to a medium mixing bowl; purée thoroughly with an immersion blender.

Rum Sauce

1　pound (4 sticks) unsalted butter
1/3　cup dark brown sugar, packed
1/2　tablespoon vanilla extract
1/4　cup rum
1/4　cup heavy cream

Add the butter to a medium saucepan set over medium heat. Add the sugar and vanilla, mixing constantly until butter is melted. Remove the pan from the heat, add the rum, and ignite with a long kitchen match. When the flames die down, add the cream immediately and whisk vigorously until sauce is completely smooth. Set aside in a warm place.

Whatcha Know Good?

In the early 1950s, New Orleans was the major port of entry for bananas shipped from Central and South America, and Brennan's restaurant Chef Paul Blange was charged with creating a dish with the popular, abundant fruit. The restaurant then named the dessert for a local businessman. The dish has become so entrenched in the local culinary canon as to now be inspiring evolutionary offshoots. This is one of them. Other riffs on the original include Bananas Foster Ice Cream, Bananas Foster Crème Brulée, and Bananas Foster King Cake. The recent return of bananas to the port following a 40-year hiatus will undoubtedly lead to a resurgence in the impact of the tropical fruit on our cuisine.

Louisiana Lime Pie with a Rye-Kissed Crust

Chef Jessica Stokes, Maurepas Foods

Zesty lime juice is best for this recipe, but any fresh citrus juice and zest will work well, too. Just use whatever is fresh at the market or from the arbor.

1 1/2 cups Graham Cracker Crumbs (recipe follows)
    Heaping 1/4 cup sugar
    Salt
6 tablespoon unsalted butter, melted, cooled
1 cup freshly squeezed lime juice
    Zest of 3 limes
7 egg yolks
2 2/3 cups sweetened condensed milk
    Whipped cream for serving

Preheat oven to 350°F.

Combine the cracker crumbs, sugar, a pinch of salt, and butter to form a crumbly mixture. Press mixture firmly across the bottom and up the sides of a nine-inch pie plate. Bake until light golden, about eight minutes. Set aside to cool.

Reduce the oven temperature to 325°F.

Whisk to combine the lime juice and zest, egg yolks, and condensed milk. Pour the mixture into the cooled crust and bake until the center is almost set, about twenty minutes. The surface of the pie will have a wrinkled appearance. Chill on a wire rack until the pie reaches room temperature, then refrigerate overnight. Serve with whipped cream.

Crisp Cinnamon Graham Crackers

The addition of rye flour gives these lightly sweet crackers a sexy little je ne sais quoi.

3/4 cup all-purpose flour
1 cup whole wheat pastry flour
1/2 cup rye flour
1/2 cup plus 3 tablespoons sugar
1 teaspoon baking powder
1/2 teaspoon baking soda
1 teaspoon salt
1 teaspoon cinnamon
1 stick unsalted butter, chilled, cut into cubes
2 tablespoons honey
2 tablespoons molasses
1/4 cup water
1 teaspoon vanilla

Sift together the flours, 1/2 cup of sugar, the baking powder and soda, salt, and half a teaspoon of the cinnamon. Add the mixture to a food processor with the butter and process until the mixture looks like coarse flakes.

Combine the honey, molasses, water, and vanilla. Blend thoroughly.

Combine the remaining 3 tablespoons sugar with 1/2 teaspoon of cinnamon. Set aside.

With the processor running, trickle in the honey mixture and pulse until combined. Dump out the mixture and knead to blend thoroughly. Divide the mixture into two logs, wrap in waxed paper, and chill until solid and cold.

Heat oven to 350°F.

Slice logs into quarter-inch discs. Lay on a greased cookie sheet two inches apart; flatten each slice gently with the palm of your hand and sprinkle with reserved cinnamon and sugar mixture. Bake until light golden, about nine minutes.

Cool and process the crackers into crumbs in a food processor.

Ooey Gooey Cake

Chef Nealy Frentz, Lola, Covington

Homey-looking Ooey Gooey Cake is most commonly found cut in squares and wrapped in plastic or cellophane next to the cash register at Louisiana gas stations. I just love that Nealy Frentz has the gumption to serve it, with great fanfare no less, in her stylish downtown Covington hotspot.

Serves 8

1   18.25-ounce box yellow cake mix (yes, boxed mix)
1   large egg
1   stick unsalted butter, melted
    Ooey Gooey Filling (recipe follows)
    Confectioners' sugar, for dusting

Preheat oven to 350°F. Grease an 8 x 8-inch square pan.

Blend the cake mix, egg, and butter in mixing bowl. Press the crumbly mixture on the bottom and up the sides of the pan. Spread the filling over the crumb mixture in the pan. Bake until golden brown and firm, about forty-five minutes to one hour. Cool for thirty minutes and dust with confectioners' sugar before serving.

Ooey Gooey Filling

Makes about 2 cups

1   stick salted butter, melted
8   ounces softened cream cheese
2   large eggs
2   teaspoons vanilla extract
1   1-pound box confectioners' sugar

Combine butter, cream cheese, eggs, vanilla, and sugar in a mixing bowl and beat until smooth.

Whatcha Know Good?

Commonly found at Southern gas stations, this gooey butter cake originated in St. Louis as an accident during the Great Depression when a German-American baker who was trying to make a typical cake batter goofed and reversed the proportions of butter and flour.

The mistake wasn't caught until after the cakes came out of the proof box. As a matter of thrift, rather than throw them away the bakery sold the delicious, yet not-so-attractive confection that has become a homey classic.

Molten Chocolate Cake with Chicory Coffee Sauce and Sweet Cashew Cream (Vegan)

Chef Anne Churchill, Bhava

If Meyer lemons are out of season, the juice and zest from of a small orange may be substituted in this vegan-friendly recipe.

When making the ganache, follow the instructions exactly: Air needs to be able to escape from the blender. If the cover is fully secured, it will blast off when you start to process the mixture and molten chocolate will go everywhere. If you keep the lid loose and do not cover it with a dish towel, you will then be taking a bath in the molten chocolate.

Makes 8 small cakes

1 1/2 cups all-purpose flour
1/2 cup unsweetened cocoa powder (Chef Churchill likes Onyx)
1 teaspoon baking powder
1/2 teaspoon kosher salt
4 ounces silken tofu
3/4 cup pure coconut, soy, or almond milk
3/4 cup maple syrup and/or agave (Chef Churchill uses a half-and-half blend)
3 tablespoons raw Louisiana cane sugar, such as Three Brothers
1/2 cup vegetable oil
1 tablespoon vanilla extract
1/2 teaspoon Meyer lemon juice
1/2 teaspoon Meyer lemon zest
Vegetable shortening or vegan margarine
Ganache (recipe follows)
Coffee and Chicory Sauce (recipe follows)
Sweet Cashew Cream (recipe follows)

Preheat the oven to 350°F.

Sift together the flour, cocoa powder, baking powder, and salt. Set aside.

Combine the tofu, milk, syrup, sugar, vegetable oil, vanilla, juice, and zest in a blender and process until fully blended and liquefied.

Combine the wet and dry ingredients and whisk until just blended. Do not over-mix or the cake will be dry.

Grease a muffin tin with vegetable shortening or vegan margarine. Fill the tins a third of the way full with cake batter. Use a melon baller or two teaspoons to form balls of ganache. Tuck one ball into the center of each muffin tin. Complete filling the tins with the remainder of the batter. Bake the cakes until they begin to pull away from the sides of the tins and the tops are just set, fifteen to eighteen minutes.

Cool the cakes slightly, then carefully invert the muffin tin. Serve the cakes with Coffee and Chicory Sauce and Sweet Cashew Cream.

Ganache

Makes 1 1/2 cups

1/2 cup 100 percent cocoa chips or pieces
Pinch of kosher salt
3/4 cup thick coconut creamer or soy milk
1/3 cup raw Louisiana cane sugar, such as Three Brothers

Put cocoa chips and salt in a blender. Set aside.

Heat the milk and sugar in a small sauce pot over medium heat until the sugar has completely dissolved. Pour the milk mixture into blender. Cover, but leave a little ventilation. Place a kitchen towel over the blender lid. Pulse the blender gently at first, then proceed to high speed to fully blend the ganache. Adjust with a little milk if necessary.

Coffee and Chicory Sauce

3 tablespoons French Market Coffee and Chicory or CDM (Note: if using another variety increase to 4 tablespoons)
2 cups cold water
1/2 cup sugar
2 tablespoons corn starch
1 teaspoon vanilla
1/2 teaspoon salt

Combine coffee, water, sugar, and corn starch in a saucepan over high heat. Bring to a boil. Stir in vanilla and salt. Remove from heat and let stand for five minutes. Pass the liquid through a French coffee press or very fine sieve. Keep warm.

Sweet Cashew Cream

2 cups raw cashews, soaked in 2 cups water for 8 hours or overnight, drained
Powdered sugar to taste
Pinch of salt
1/2 teaspoon vanilla

Combine cashews, sugar, salt, and vanilla in a blender and process until creamy. Adjust sweetness as desired.

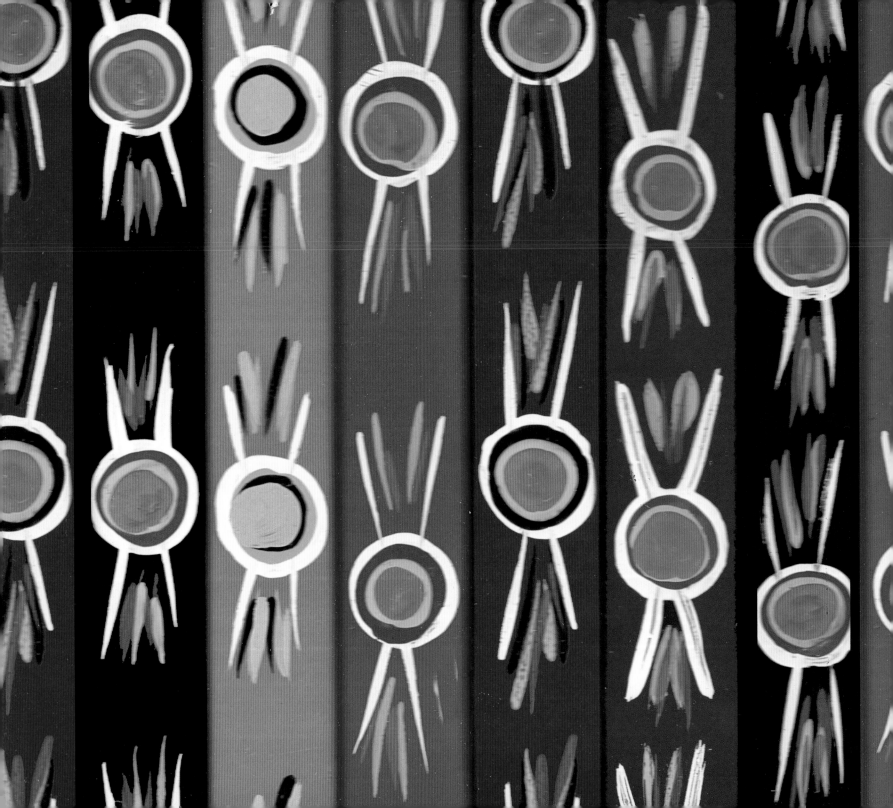

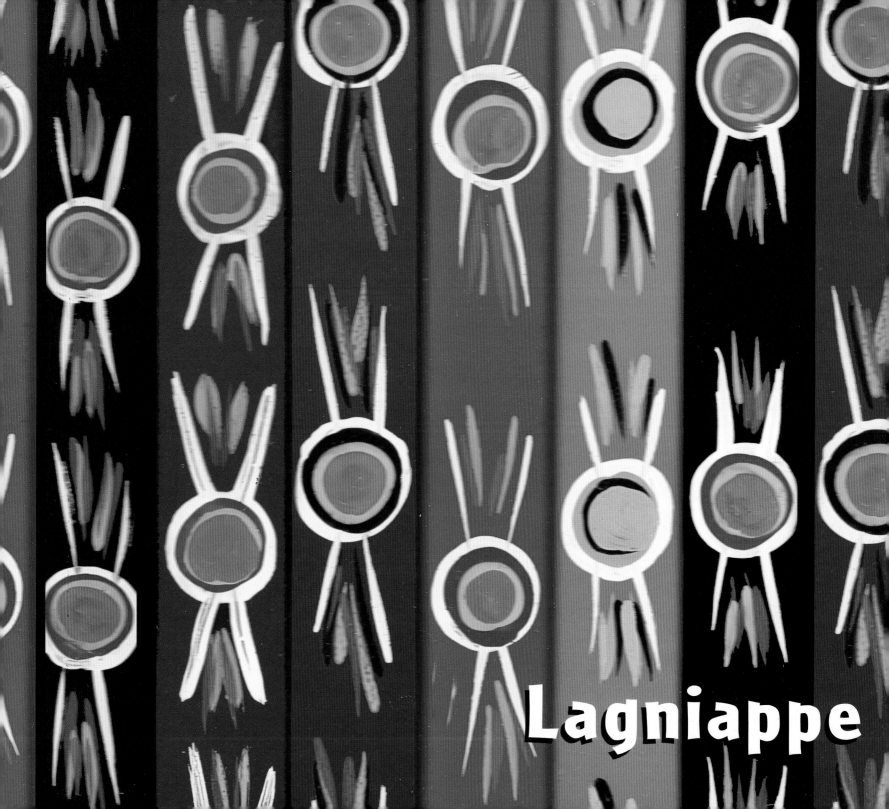

Lagniappe

Rustic Roasted Garlic Bread

See Butter Bean Hummus recipe, p. 17

Makes 1 loaf

3	cups all-purpose flour	1/2	cup peeled garlic cloves
1 3/4	teaspoons kosher salt	1/2	teaspoon sea salt
1/2	teaspoon yeast	1	tablespoon olive oil
1 1/2	cups water	1	teaspoon herbs de Provence

Whisk to combine flour, salt, and yeast in a large mixing bowl. Add water and mix with a wooden spoon until a shaggy mixture forms. Cover bowl with plastic wrap and place in a warm location to rise for at least twelve hours or overnight.

Preheat the oven to 375°F.

Toss the garlic with the salt, olive oil, and herbs de Provence in a small baking dish. Roast the garlic until light golden, fifteen to twenty minutes. Cool.

Cut a piece of parchment paper to fit the bottom of an oven-safe clay pot or covered enameled Dutch oven. Flour parchment paper and set aside.

Place the pot or Dutch oven in the oven. Turn heat to 450°F., so pot and oven are heating at the same time.

Meanwhile, dump the dough onto a heavily floured surface and flatten into a disc of about eight inches. Scrape the garlic and herbs atop the disc and fold the sides in to enclose the garlic. Flip the dough over, seam side down, and shape roughly into a ball. Use a sharp knife to cut some slashes or a hash pattern in the top of the dough. When oven reaches 450°F., remove hot pot from oven, carefully insert the parchment, place the dough atop, and replace the lid. Place the Dutch oven back in the oven for thirty minutes, then remove the lid and bake until golden and fabulous, about twenty minutes more.

Remove the bread from the pot and cool on a rack if you can stand to wait that long.

MoPho Mayo

See Crispy Fried Oysters with MoPho Mayo recipe, p. 15

Makes 2 cups

2 cups best-quality mayonnaise (Chef Gulotta likes Blue Plate)
1 tablespoon fermented red pepper paste (may substitute Sriracha)
1 tablespoon rice wine vinegar
1 teaspoon fish sauce
2 cloves garlic, minced

Combine mayonnaise, red pepper paste, vinegar, fish sauce, and garlic. Chill at least one hour to marry flavors.

Oyster Dredge

See Crispy Fried Oysters with MoPho Mayo recipe, p. 15

Makes 2 quarts

2	cups rice flour	1	tablespoon garlic powder
2	cups corn flour	1	teaspoon celery salt
2	cups cornmeal	1	teaspoon black pepper
2	cups all-purpose flour	1	teaspoon Korean red pepper flakes (may substitute crushed red pepper)
2	cups panko bread crumbs, pulsed in blender		

Combine flours, bread crumbs, garlic powder, celery salt, and peppers in a large bowl. Mix thoroughly

Pickled Blue Cheese Vinaigrette

See Crispy Fried Oysters with MoPho Mayo recipe, p. 15

Makes about 2 cups

1 clove garlic, minced
1/2 teaspoon grated fresh ginger, plus additional to taste
1/2 Thai chile, seeded and minced
1 1/2 cups oil (canola, vegetable, or any neutral oil may be used)
1 teaspoon soy sauce
1/2 cup rice wine vinegar
1 teaspoon fish sauce
2 tablespoons minced yellow onion
1/4 teaspoon Korean red pepper flakes (may substitute crushed red pepper)
2 tablespoons minced Daikon radish
Sesame oil to taste
4 ounces blue cheese crumbled

In a medium saucepan over medium heat, toast the garlic, ginger, and fresh chile in 1 tablespoon of the canola oil until fragrant, about two minutes. Add the soy sauce, rice wine vinegar, and fish sauce. Remove from heat. Once the mixture has reached room temperature, whisk in the remaining canola oil, pepper flakes, onion, and radish. Season to taste with sesame oil, freshly grated ginger, and a little more fish sauce and vinegar if desired.

Once the vinaigrette is completely cooled, add the crumbled blue cheese and marinate overnight in the refrigerator.

Pickled Carrot Ribbons

See Cumin and Cilantro Pork Sausage Hand Pies with Satsuma Crème Fraiche recipe, p. 21

Makes 1 quart

- 1 cup unfiltered apple cider vinegar
- 1/2 cup Mirin or other sweet white wine
- 1/2 cup water
- 1 1/4 tablespoons salt
- 1 1/4 tablespoons sugar
- 4 sprigs fresh thyme
- 1 very large carrot, peeled into thin ribbons with a vegetable peeler

Combine vinegar, wine, water, salt, and sugar in a sauce pot. Bring to a simmer and cook until sugar and salt have dissolved. Remove from heat and cool.

Add the carrot ribbons and thyme sprigs to a one-quart jar. Pour in the cooled brine and seal the jar. Store in the refrigerator.

Simple Rustic Crusty Bread

Langlois Culinary Crossroads

The appearance and texture of this bread are what compel people to fork over big bucks for bread. Golden, rugged and chewy, when presented with a mousse, paté, a hunk of cheese or just a pat of good butter this will take you, sans airfare, straight to the Old World. The best part? It's made with four cheap ingredients, requires no messy kneading, and you just can't screw it up.

See Chicken Liver Mousse recipe, p. 27

Makes 1 loaf

- 3 cups all-purpose flour
- 1 3/4 teaspoons kosher salt
- 1/2 teaspoon yeast
- 1 1/2 cups water

Whisk to combine flour, salt, and yeast into a large mixing bowl. Add water and mix with a wooden spoon until a shaggy mixture forms. Cover bowl with plastic wrap and place in a warm location to rise for at least twelve hours or overnight.

Cut a piece of parchment paper to fit the bottom of an oven-safe clay pot or covered enameled Dutch oven. Flour the parchment paper and set aside.

Place the covered clay pot or Dutch oven in the oven. Turn heat to 450°F., so pot and oven are heating at the same time. Meanwhile,

dump the dough onto a heavily floured surface and shape it roughly into a ball. Use a sharp knife to cut some slashes or a hash pattern in the top of the dough. When oven reaches 450°F., remove pot from oven, carefully insert parchment, toss in the dough, and replace the lid. Place back in the oven for thirty minutes, then remove the lid and bake until golden and fabulous, about twenty minutes. Remove the bread from the pot and cool it on a rack.

Cashew Purée

See Market Vegetable Salad recipe, p. 37

Makes 1 cup

1 cup raw cashews
1 cup water
Sea salt to taste

Soak the cashews in water for at least two hours, preferably overnight. Pour the water and softened cashews into a blender and purée until completely smooth. Season with sea salt. Chill.

Black Olive Praline

See Market Vegetable Salad recipe, p. 37

- 5 1/2 tablespoons sugar
- 5 1/2 tablespoons liquid glucose (available in crafts stores, such as Michael's, under the brand name Wilton)
- 3 ounces dehydrated pitted black olives, chopped

In a small saucepan, mix the sugar and glucose and cook over low heat, stirring constantly until the mixture is a deep amber color. Immediately stir in the dried olives.

Pour the mixture onto a sheet pan lined with wax paper. Cool completely. Chop finely with a chef's knife. Store in a sealed container.

Short Rib Marinade

See Grilled Short Ribs recipe, p. 43

Makes 3 1/2 cups

- 1   1-inch piece Chinese cinnamon
- 1   tablespoon Szechwan pepper
- 1/2   cup soy sauce
- 3   cups Mirin
- 3   tablespoons palm sugar or granulated sugar
-     Zest of 2 limes
- 4   cloves garlic, minced

In a medium pot over medium heat, stir cinnamon, pepper, soy sauce, Mirin, sugar, zest, and garlic together until sugar dissolves. Cool.

Short Rib Glaze

See Grilled Short Ribs recipe, p. 43

Makes 2 cups

- 1/2   tablespoon shrimp paste
- 1   clove garlic, minced
- 1   tablespoon peeled, grated fresh ginger
- 1/4   cup canola oil
- 1   cup Short Rib Marinade (see above)
- 1   tablespoon fish sauce
-     Zest and juice of 1 lime
- 1/4   cup hoisin sauce
- 1/4   cup honey

In a medium sauce pot over medium heat, toast the shrimp paste, garlic, and ginger in the canola oil until it is caramelized, about four minutes. Add the marinade, fish sauce, lime zest and juice, hoisin sauce, and honey and simmer for eight minutes.

Ginger Vinaigrette

See Grilled Short Ribs recipe, p. 43

Makes 2 1/4 cups

- 1 1/2   cups canola oil
- 1   French shallot, minced
- 1   2-inch piece fresh ginger, peeled and grated
- 1   clove garlic, minced
- 1/2   cup seasoned rice wine vinegar
- 1   teaspoon Korean red pepper flake (may substitute crushed red pepper)
-     Sugar to taste
-     Salt to taste

In a medium bowl, mix oil, shallot, ginger, garlic, vinegar, pepper, sugar, and salt together but do not emulsify. Check for flavor and if desired, add more oil or vinegar to taste. Set aside.

Esses' Kosher Dills

No jarring and processing necessary: These refrigerator pickles marinate in a covered container in the refrigerator. Start the pickles one week before you plan to use them.

See Lamb Sliders recipe, p. 49

Makes 1 Quart

- 1 1/2   cups water
- 3/4   cup white vinegar
- 1   teaspoon dill seed
- 2   teaspoons kosher salt
- 2   tablespoons sugar
- 2   teaspoons brown mustard seed
- 1   teaspoon chili flakes
- 1/2   bunch fresh dill, chopped
- 1   full head garlic, smashed
- 1   pound small washed Kirby cucumbers, scrubbed

Combine water, vinegar, dill, salt, sugar, mustard seed, and chili flakes in a large sauce pot set over high heat. Bring to a boil and cook until the sugar and salt have dissolved. Remove from the heat and cool until slightly warm.

Add the cucumbers, garlic, and dill to a large lidded plastic or glass container. Pour the brine over the cucumbers. Allow the cucumbers to soak in the brine for one week. Will keep, refrigerated, for three weeks.

Creamy Stone-Ground Grits

As divine as it is, mascarpone can be hard to find and it's always expensive. To make a highly passable fake, blend 8 ounces softened cream cheese with 1/2 cup sour cream and 1/4 cup heavy cream. Use half for this recipe and reserve the rest for another use.

See Cast-Iron Chicken Fricassee recipe, p. 51

Makes about 4 cups

- 3 cups water
- 3 cups heavy cream
  - Salt
- 1 teaspoon white pepper
- 1 teaspoon granulated garlic
- 4 tablespoons unsalted butter
- 1 1/2 cups yellow stone-ground grits
- 1/2 cup mascarpone cheese

Combine water, cream, salt, pepper, garlic, and butter in a sauce pot or Dutch oven; bring to a boil. Reduce the heat to low, add the grits, and cook until liquid has absorbed, twenty to thirty minutes. Stir in mascarpone.

Braised Collard Greens

See Cast-Iron Chicken Fricassee recipe, p. 51

Serves 6 to 8 as a side dish

- 1 pound smoked bacon, diced
  - Rendered bacon fat
- 1 yellow onion, diced
- 6 cloves garlic, minced
- 2 quarts chicken stock
- 1/4 cup sugar (optional)
- 1/4 cup Steen's cane vinegar
  - Salt and freshly ground black pepper
  - 4 bunches collard greens, washed and chopped

Render the bacon in a large sauce pot or Dutch oven, preferably cast iron. Remove the bacon and reserve. Add enough additional bacon fat to equal 1 cup.

Add the onion and garlic and cook until onions are translucent, about five minutes. Add the stock, sugar, vinegar, salt, and pepper. Bring to a boil. Add the greens, cover, and cook until tender, about one hour. Serve topped with reserved bacon.

Lamb Sausage Gravy

This is also delicious over hot biscuits and can be made with 1 pound of crumbled best-quality pork sausage.

See Chicken-Fried Sweetbreads recipe, p. 53

Makes about 3 cups

- 1 pound Lamb Sausage (recipe follows) or high-quality pork sausage, casings removed, crumbled
- 8 tablespoons all-purpose flour
- 3 cups whole milk
- 1 teaspoon kosher salt
- 1 teaspoon black pepper

Brown the sausage over medium-high heat in a heavy sauce pot or Dutch oven. Add the flour and cook for one minute, stirring constantly. Pour in the milk, season with the salt and pepper, and bring mixture almost to a boil, watching carefully. Reduce the heat to a simmer and cook until the gravy is thick and the floury taste is gone.

Lamb Sausage

This recipe makes more than you will need for the gravy dish, but it freezes well and can be crumbled to make meatballs or formed into patties and fried off for a divine brunch treat.

To make a pork sausage, substitute 5 pounds of pork shoulder (Boston butt for the lamb), omit the rosemary, and double the amount of sage.

See Chicken-Fried Sweetbreads recipe, p. 53

Makes 5 pounds

- 5 pounds lamb shoulder, cut into strips
- 2 tablespoons kosher salt
- 1 tablespoon black pepper
- 1/2 ounce chopped fresh rosemary
- 1/4 ounce chopped fresh sage
- 1 teaspoon cayenne
- 2 teaspoons red pepper flakes
- 2 tablespoons light brown sugar
- 1 tablespoon plus 1 teaspoon chopped garlic
- 1 tablespoons plus 1 teaspoon Creole mustard

Combine lamb, salt, pepper, rosemary, sage, cayenne, pepper, sugar, garlic, and mustard and pass through a meat grinder.

Pickled Mustard Greens

This recipe makes more than you will need for the sweetbread presentation, but the mustard greens are also a wonderful, piquant addition to pork chops, sandwiches, and as a garnish on just about anything for a bit of quick Southern flair.

See Chicken-Fried Sweetbreads recipe, p. 53

Makes four 1-quart jars

- 4 pounds mustard greens, cleaned and trimmed
- 8 cups cider vinegar
- 3 cups water
- 2 tablespoons salt
- 4 tablespoons sugar
- 6 cloves garlic, peeled
- 8 tablespoons mustard seeds
- 1/2 onion thinly sliced

In a large pot, bring the vinegar, water, salt, and sugar to a boil. Add the mustard greens and cook until fully wilted. Divide the garlic, mustard seeds, and onion evenly among four sterilized jars. Divide the mustard greens among the jars and top with pot liquor, leaving a half-inch of head space in each jar. Seal each jar with a new lid and process in boiling water for fifteen minutes.

Braised Pork Trotters

See Pork Trotter Gumbo recipe, p. 55

- 2 tablespoons vegetable oil
- 2 yellow onions, chopped
- 3 celery ribs, chopped
- 1 large carrot or 2 small, chopped
- 4 bay leaves
- 1 tablespoon black pepper
- 1 tablespoon kosher salt
- 10 sprigs thyme
- 4 cloves garlic, minced
- 5 pork trotters (pig's feet)
- 2 to 3 quarts chicken stock, preferably homemade

Heat the oil in a large cast-iron Dutch oven over medium heat. Add the onions and cook until slightly brown, about ten minutes. Add the celery, carrot, bay leaves, pepper and salt, thyme, and garlic and continue to cook until lightly caramelized, about ten minutes.

Add the pork trotters and enough stock to cover them. Bring to a boil, reduce the heat to very low, and simmer until tender, about three

hours. Remove the Dutch oven from the heat. Allow to rest until the trotters are cool enough to handle. Remove the trotters and set aside. Strain the stock, discard the vegetables, and set the stock aside. Pick the meat from the bones, checking carefully for small bones.

Deviled Eggs

See Pork Trotter Gumbo recipe, p. 55

Makes 10 pieces

- 5 large eggs
- 2 tablespoons best-quality mayonnaise (Chef Stolzfus likes Blue Plate)
- 2 teaspoons sour cream
- 1 teaspoon Dijon mustard
- 1 teaspoon Crystal hot sauce
- 1/4 teaspoon kosher salt

Add the eggs to a sauce pot in a single layer. Cover with cold water and set the pot over high heat. Bring the water to a boil and cook at a full boil for ten minutes.

Shock the eggs in ice water. When cool enough to handle, gently peel the eggs and cut in half vertically. Remove the yolks. Set the whites aside.

Push the yolks through a fine mesh strainer into a mixing bowl. Add mayonnaise, sour cream, Dijon mustard, hot sauce, and salt and beat with a wooden spoon until smooth. Correct the seasoning as desired.

Add the yolk mixture to a piping bag or to a zip-top plastic bag with a corner snipped off and pipe the mixture neatly into the reserved halved egg whites.

Preserved Lemons

Spices such as clove, coriander seeds, peppercorns, cinnamon stick, or bay leaves may be added to the lemons as they are packed in the jar.

See Naked Veal with Fried Oysters recipe, p. 59

Makes 1 quart

 Salt
8 to 10 lemons (preferably Meyer), scrubbed very clean
 1/4 cup freshly squeezed lemon juice, if needed
 Sterilized quart canning jar

Spoon 2 tablespoons salt into the bottom of the jar.

For each lemon, cut off any protruding stems and cut 1/4 inch off the tip. Cut each as if cutting in half lengthwise, starting from the tip, but do not cut all the way through; keep the lemon intact at the base. Turn the lemon a half turn and make another cut in a similar manner, so the lemon is quartered, but again, attached at the base.

Pull the lemons open and generously salt both insides and out.

Pack the lemons in the jar, forcing them down so the juice is extracted and rises to the top. Continue filling the jar with lemons, making sure the top is covered with lemon juice. Add more fresh-squeezed juice as necessary. Top with 2 tablespoons salt.

Seal the jar and refrigerate for three weeks, occasionally turning the jar upside down until the lemon rinds soften.

To use, remove a lemon from the jar and rinse thoroughly in water to remove the salt. Discard the seeds before using.

Will keep, refrigerated, for up to six months.

Cane Syrup Gastrique

See Toups' Double-Cut Pork Chops recipe, p. 75

Makes 1 cup

1 cup Steen's Cane Syrup
1 cup Steen's Cane Vinegar

Combine the syrup and vinegar in a sauce pot set over medium heat. Bring to a boil, reduce heat to medium-low, and cook until mixture is reduced by half, about ten minutes.

Pretzel Bread

See Pretzel Bread Pudding recipe, p. 107

Makes 2 7-inch loaves

 1 cup milk
 2 tablespoons unsalted butter
1/4 teaspoon vanilla extract
 1 envelope yeast
 2 tablespoons dark brown sugar
 2 teaspoons salt
 3 cups all-purpose flour or more as needed
 3 quarts water
3/4 cup baking soda
 1 egg whisked with 1 teaspoon water

Add the milk, butter, and vanilla extract to a saucepan set over medium heat and heat to 110°F. The butter will not completely melt. Pour the mixture into a large mixing bowl; add the yeast and the brown sugar. Stir in the salt and 2 cups of flour, and beat for three minutes.

Gradually add enough additional flour to make a soft dough. Dump the dough onto a floured surface and knead until it is smooth and elastic, about eight to ten minutes. Place in a greased bowl, cover with a damp towel, and allow to rest until doubled in size, about four hours.

Preheat the oven to 400°F.

Combine the water and the baking soda in a large pot and bring to a boil. Punch the dough down and divide into two equal pieces. Form each piece into a tight, smooth ball. Boil each loaf in the solution for two minutes, turning after one minute. Remove the loaves from the pot using a slotted spoon and place on a greased baking sheet.

Brush the loaves with the egg wash and cut a cross in the top of each. Bake for fifteen minutes, then reduce the temperature to 350°F and bake until the loaves are evenly browned, about ten to twelve minutes more.

Remove the loaves to cool on a wire rack.

Index

Acknowledgements

My cup runneth over for my friend, mentor, and colleague, Kit Wohl, for handing me seeds of inspiration, then tirelessly and patiently holding up the lantern while I planted a garden in the dark; and for Sam Hanna and his masterful ability to capture and manipulate a quality of light that makes everything beautiful.

A heartfelt merci beaucoup to the talented and clever Simon Hardeveld, aka. Simon of New Orleans, for the use of his whimsical, distinctive artwork, which epitomizes the fun and funky side of today's New Orleans.

I offer my gratitude to my affiliates and colleagues in the Cookbook Studio—Barry Garner, Eloisa Zepeda, Meredith Leber, and Chef Zach Engel—for your assistance and enthusiasm.

I lift my spoon to Amberly Zapada and Billy Wohl, our charming and enthusiastic test kitchen cheerleaders; we revel in their delight at sharing new taste sensations and perfecting time-honored ones.

I adore the many chefs and restaurateurs who joined us in the kitchen to share their recipes, skills, and stories. Your generosity is humbling. I hope you are well served here.

Abundant appreciation is due to the keen eyes of text editor Cathy Ritter; the enduring patience and skill of Michael Lauve, our art director; and to Liz Williams of the Southern Food & Beverage Institute for her golden pen and encyclopedic knowledge of Louisiana's culinary culture.

A hearty "Here, Here!" to Poppy Tooker and Robert Peyton for their friendship, encouragement, and moral support.

Thank you to Kathleen Nettleton and Nina Kooij of Pelican Publishing for this opportunity and for their guidance through this process.